IMAGES

A CREATIVE DIGITAL WORKFLOW FOR GRAPHIC DESIGNERS

Dedicated to Jack Seddon, who taught me that there are no problems, only solutions.

IMAGES

A CREATIVE DIGITAL WORKFLOW FOR GRAPHIC DESIGNERS

Tony Seddon

with contributions
by Robert Clymo

RotoVision

A RotoVision Book

Published and distributed by RotoVision SA
Route Suisse 9
CH-1295 Mies
Switzerland

RotoVision SA
Sales and Editorial Office
Sheridan House, 114 Western Road
Hove BN3 1DD, UK

Tel: +44 (0)1273 72 72 68
Fax: +44 (0)1273 72 72 69
www.rotovision.com

10 9 8 7 6 5 4 3 2 1

ISBN: 978-2-940361-47-2

Design and art direction: Tony Seddon

Typeset in Palatino and Griffith Gothic

Printed in Singapore by Star Standard Industries (Pte.) Ltd.

A word about software

This book isn't intended to be seen as a missing manual, and isn't attempting to recommend any one product over another. Therefore, if you don't own the application that's used to illustrate a point, it's highly probable that you'll be able to achieve the same thing using another comparable application. This also applies to the operating system of your choice, and every effort has been made to ensure that the methods discussed can be implemented using software available for both Mac OSX and Windows.

Contents

1479_Book artwork

15 items, 17.51 GB available

Name

1479-Image.0_001–007.indd
1479-Image.1_008–015.indd
1479-Image.2_016–027.indd
1479-Image.3_028–047.indd
1479-Image.4_048–079.indd
1479-Image.4_080–099.indd
1479-Image.4_100–119.indd
1479-Image.4_120–135.indd
1479-Image.5_136–157.indd
1479-Image.6_158–167.indd
1479-Image.7_168–179.indd
1479-Image.7_180–191.indd
1479-Image.8_192–203.indd
1479-Image.9_204–215.indd
1479-Image.end_216–224.indd

Introduction

So—about this "creative digital workflow for graphic designers." Deep down we all know that it's something we should try to think about, but more often than not we manage to find something that *appears* to be more interesting, or more rewarding or, the worst excuse of all, more urgent.

Graphic designers in particular are vulnerable to the temptations of ignoring the importance of the thoughtful preparation and planning of complex projects. We get excited about the creative process we are going to embark upon and forget to think about that part of the project which comprises editing, naming, preparing, distributing, and finally storing the building blocks of graphic design—the vital images.

You may already have a method that seems to work pretty well, but on analysis does it really work as well as it should? Was the working method you follow designed, or did it evolve around a series of projects and the various problems they presented at the time? There are many different ways to get the job done, and people will invariably approach each project differently, but there are underlying principles which can help you to avoid problems.

The aim of this book is to provide you with the information you need to form a *method* and a *philosophy* for building your own creative digital workflow, improving image management and therefore freeing up more time for creativity. It also takes you through typical design and artwork preparation stages for both print and online projects, with an emphasis on how images are handled. If you routinely struggle to focus on the aspects of running or collaborating on creative projects (and we all do), this book may be just what you need.

Observing a creative digital workflow doesn't have to be a chore, despite what some people will tell you. Jonathan Kenyon of Vault 49 (www.vault49.com) says:

"We consider our *business* as being image management, it being a broader term for art direction fused with original creations. This applies whether the image is created entirely by our own hands, or whether the design involves the collaborative talents of many of our contributors."

I think he's right. If seen as an integral part of the design process, and indeed if approached with a creative spirit, managing your project successfully can be almost as rewarding an experience as the design process itself.

Tony Seddon

➲ Which image is the right one for the job? How much will the image cost? Where did the images come from and who shot them? Whose permission do I need? How do I make sure the image will reproduce perfectly? All will be revealed.
Photography: Jason Keith

Establishing an image-preparation workflow

What's so important about an image workflow, and why do you need to have one at all? Well, it's obviously up to you to decide if establishing an image workflow can be of benefit to you, but I'm going to stick my neck out here and say that I'm certain it will be. If you've ever got to the end of a design project only to discover that you can't find all the images, or that some of your images aren't the correct resolution for high-quality reproduction (even though you thought they were), or indeed that your carefully planned schedule has unravelled and half of your high-resolution images haven't even arrived, read on. This book is for you.

What is a workflow & why have one?

Put simply, a workflow is the management and movement of specific project-related tasks through a work process. It's about how the tasks are structured, how they're completed, who completes them, how they are prioritized, what time frame they need to be completed in, and ultimately how they are synchronized to create a single product at a specific time.

More specifically, a workflow can represent the creation and management of a creative project's content. In the context of this book I'll be discussing workflows as visual representations of the tasks and actions outlined in that short introductory paragraph, paying particular attention to how images are created, managed, and used in print and web projects.

When asked, "Why do you need a workflow?" my usual answer is, "Why would you not want to have a workflow?" Whenever I embark on a new project I get nervous if I don't have a good understanding of how the individual strands of the project will come together. For example, I always want to know what I should expect to receive from a photographer or illustrator, the format in which the material will be provided, and when I can realistically expect it to arrive. I take a similar approach with text. Will it indicate where images are supposed to go? Will it be complete? Has it been edited?

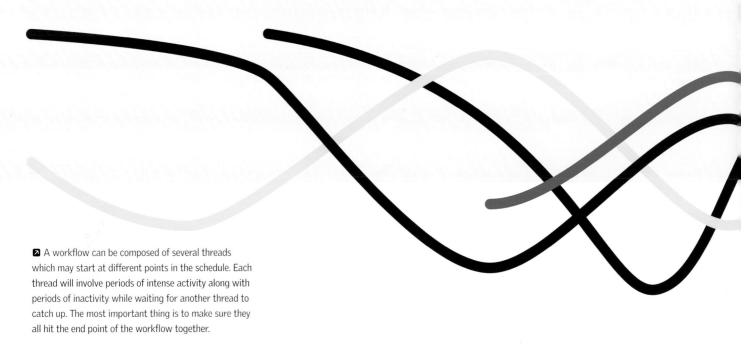

↗ A workflow can be composed of several threads which may start at different points in the schedule. Each thread will involve periods of intense activity along with periods of inactivity while waiting for another thread to catch up. The most important thing is to make sure they all hit the end point of the workflow together.

The benefits of a workflow

Creating a workflow has two main benefits. The first is that it enables progress of a project to be tracked against an overall schedule. The second is that a workflow enables a designer to "optimize" every stage of a project, so ensuring the project as a whole receives a consistent and considered approach. For example, establishing a workflow will allow you to be consistent in the way you prepare images for each of your concurrently running projects. There's a good chance that over time you'll find certain key elements of a workflow work well for all your projects and can be used as the starting points for each new workflow that you create. The most important thing to remember is that once you've established a workflow for a project, you must follow it closely, just as you would if you were following a recipe in a cookery book. But "closely" is not the same as "slavishly"—there will still be times when you need to be flexible.

This combination of quality control through established rules, and consistency gained through tried and tested procedures, creates an environment where you can quickly and easily deal with the process of preparing large numbers of images for print or web projects. In turn this means you don't have to spend time thinking about what needs to be done every time you try to find and open an image on your computer. The result— increased efficiency, and therefore more time for creativity and experimentation. So that's the theory, but how is it achieved?

Establishing your image workflow

A good place to start when establishing your image workflow is to think carefully about not just the individual tasks that must be completed, but also how you would like to complete those tasks.

This may sound obvious, but in my experience designers often back themselves into a corner in order to please clients or ensure deadlines are met. This is partly due to the fact that designers are generally among the last people to work intensively on a project before it goes off to be printed or published online. For this reason, when mapping out a workflow make sure it takes into account how you prefer to approach the all-important final stages (without being too self-serving, of course), and if the workflow is working well for others but not for you,

put pressure on the team to make the necessary changes to ensure you're given a chance to do your job properly.

Identify the key stages

When establishing your workflow, think carefully about the key stages of the project you are planning. These will differ from project to project, but it's likely that there'll be some stages that are common to many of your projects. Keep records of your earlier workflows and refer back to your notes so that you can identify and therefore avoid

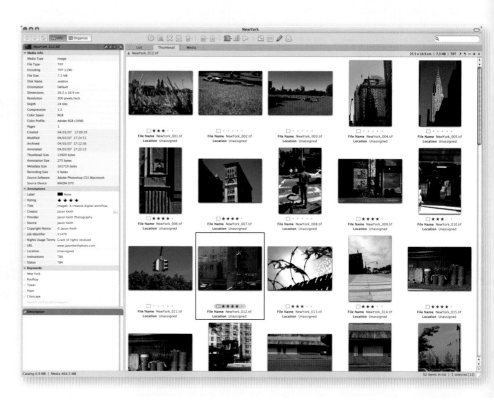

⬆ A digital catalog like the one above, made with Microsoft Expression Media (formerly iView MediaPro), will help you track the progress of all images within any given workflow.

Photography: Jason Keith

problems experienced on previous projects. Analyze the schedule carefully and allot periods of time to each task that is required. Some examples of what to consider in an image-management workflow for a typical design project could be:

→ Commissioning and briefing a specialist picture researcher.

→ Preparing a photo shoot and commissioning and briefing the photographer.

→ Art-directing the photo shoot.

→ Editing and selecting all images.

→ Cross-checking the selected images against a text manuscript or flatplan.

→ Assessing whether there are sufficient images, and ensuring budgets are adhered to.

→ Arranging any necessary additional photography or picture research, or carrying out your own additional picture research through online image libraries.

→ Briefing an illustrator and ensuring that fully annotated artwork reference is available if required.

→ Creating a secure system of project-specific folders in which to store images.

→ Ensuring all the images are filed in the correct folders.

→ Naming all the images using a system that helps to identify them and that indicates which project they belong to.

→ Creating a digital catalog of all the images relating to the project.

→ Ensuring that any necessary adjustment work on the images prior to commencing the design process is completed.

→ Preparing sample layouts to ensure design issues are finalized well in advance of the layout work commencing.

→ Briefing the designer, if work is to be outsourced. →

Prioritizing

When planning a workflow, I always advise people to concentrate on those stages of the job that they think are most likely to cause the biggest problems. It could be insufficient time or budget, or it could be something more specific to the project such as images that have to be sourced from non-professional suppliers and which will therefore need a lot of work to ensure they are of publishable quality. Once these potential problem areas are resolved, the workflow should become progressively easier to plan.

⊕ Establishing your image workflow

Identify your goal

You may have come up with a great image-management workflow, but ultimately if the end result isn't up to scratch the workflow has effectively failed. Identify the goals clearly and focus on them throughout the planning stage. It goes without saying that one of your aims will be to ensure that the reproduction of the images, be it in print or on screen, is technically of the highest possible quality. However, also give some thought to how each stage of the job can achieve the *creative* result that you want, and think about how you can use the tools at your disposal to achieve that result—whether they be a comprehensive database of images or the latest version of a software package. For example, Adobe Photoshop is undoubtedly the industry standard for use in the preparation and manipulation of images, but it is also one of the most workflow-friendly applications, through its use of actions and scripts.

Adapt to each project's needs

You can't assume that the efficient image workflow you established for one project is going to work for another, so it's important to consider a project's individual requirements. In fact, you can't even assume that every image in any one project will

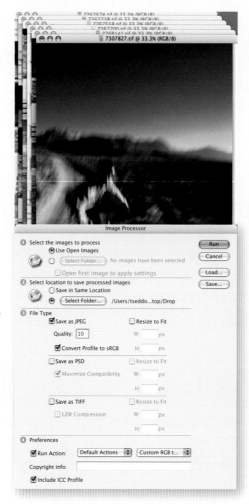

proceed through the workflow in the same way—and the stage that will generally need to remain the most flexible is the image-processing stage. There will, however, be a number of processes that you nearly always include and can build your workflow around. For example, one of the first things I do is

give a unique name to each of the images within each project to avoid overwriting files, and use an assigned code to tie them to their project. This means that if one or two images accidentally stray from their folders, I can easily locate them and move them back to their correct location. File naming is covered in more detail on pages 058–061. I also tend to stick to a broadly similar procedure when first opening any photographs that I've either shot myself or know to be uncorrected by the photographer. However, every image requiring any adjustment should be looked at individually to establish what needs to be done to achieve the best result. This is where the image workflow must be allowed a degree of flexibility. The techniques for adjusting your images are discussed in more detail throughout Chapter Four.

It's a good idea to monitor key software developments too. A new feature in the latest release of your chosen software package may completely replace a stage of your image workflow that previously had to be achieved using a more complex procedure.

⬆ An example of how workflow-friendly Photoshop is can be found in the Image Processor script [*File > Scripts > Image Processor*]. This script is supplied as part of the installed package and is very useful for simple batch conversions.

⬆ An image workflow may vary from project to project, but the stages represented here are typical of the average design project involving sourced or specially commissioned imagery.

An image workflow overview

Commission image research
either from a specialist freelance researcher or through an image-library account handler

Carry out personal image research
using an online resource such as an image library, or from accumulated reference material

Commission a photographer
ensuring that their particular specialism or personal style is suitable for the project

Commission an illustrator
ensuring that their illustrative style is suitable for the project

Attend photo shoot

Collate all images and review them using Adobe Bridge to gain an initial overview of the available choices

Edit and select images based on quality and suitability

Check images against a shot list or plan

Attend reshoot

Recommission or re-source images that are unsatisfactory

Organize and file all images within a structured system of folders
(see pages 058–061)

Rename all images using a standardized convention and convert them to your preferred format
(see pages 058–061)

Review final image selection using Adobe Bridge
adding a standardized set of basic, organizational metadata (see pages 062–065)

Create a catalog of all images that are part of the final selection, and add metadata as appropriate
using Expression Media, Extensis Portfolio, or an alternative application of your choice (see pages 072–079)

Process and adjust any images that require further attention
(see pages 100–123)

Begin design and layout

Planning & scheduling projects

When you sit down to begin work on a new design project, what's the first thing that normally happens? Do you get stuck into the creative thinking (the fun part) and hope for the best, or do you give some thought to the objectives, logistics, schedule, and budget for the project? As designers we all like to work on the ideas most of all. That's what we're trained to do, and it's why we do this job in the first place. However, if you're not organized, and are therefore difficult to work with, it doesn't matter how great your ideas are—your clients will eventually look elsewhere. This chapter provides an insight into getting the planning stage right.

Considerations

The solutions to most design problems are rarely arrived at immediately; they usually come about through a series of processes assembled by a designer or a creative team. When I sit down at the beginning of a new project to draw up the workflow, I begin by asking myself a series of standard questions.

What are the main objectives?

If you haven't worked with your client before, find out as much as you can about their business and what they want to achieve. They may have a particular market position or strategy that they wish to rigidly maintain, or they may want a complete change of direction. Either way, focus on the objectives of the project as early as you can, as this gives you both the starting point and the goal to your plan. This also applies if you are working on a brief for your own company or for yourself. Remember that the completion or delivery date is in itself a specific objective.

How will you get the job done?

Look at every possible stage of the project that you can realistically predict, and build each stage into the workflow. The image workflow itself will be one of these stages, and will run either concurrently with other stages of the project or on its own. An analysis of the completed workflow will tell you what equipment you will need, how many people you must involve, and what specific skills each team member should possess. Remember to build in as much leeway as possible to allow for the stages that you couldn't predict but which more often than not will occur.

What are the deadlines?

Ensure that a realistic schedule is established as early as possible, and be certain that you can achieve the deadlines before you sign up to them. Unless you're on extremely good terms, a client will not forgive a missed deadline that all parties had earlier agreed. However, in my experience honesty about achievable deadlines is generally respected. If you think something can't be done in two weeks but can be done in three, ask for the extra week at the planning stage and back up your request with a reasoned explanation of why you need that time. Unless there's a very compelling reason for the deadline to

⬆ When there is no leeway in a schedule, as is the case with these production posters for the Almeida Theatre, images must be sourced well in advance to meet the strict deadlines. Note also the strict adherence to layout style, providing a form of "brand recognition" for the theater's publicity.
Design: With Relish

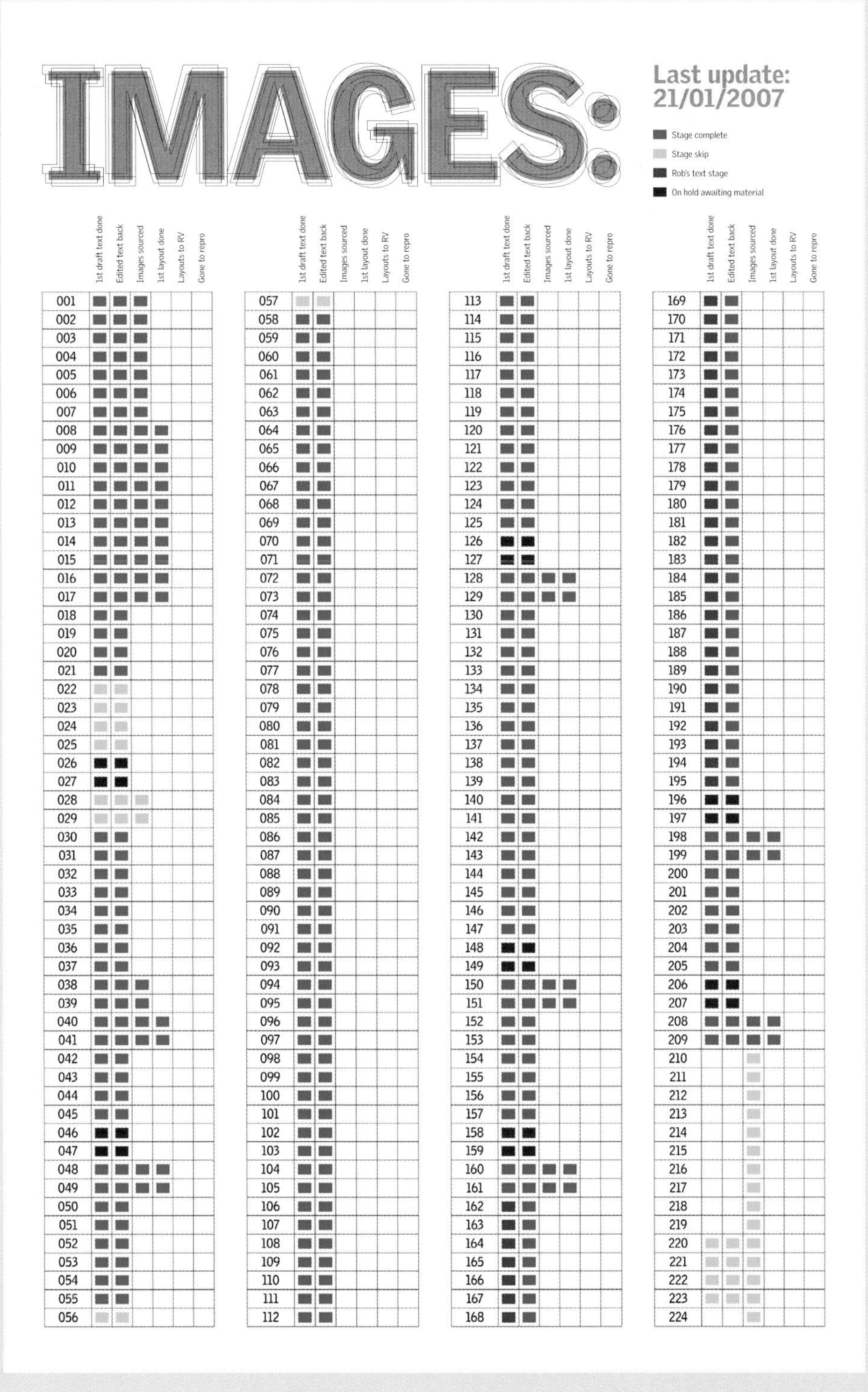

IMAGES:

Last update: 21/01/2007

- ■ Stage complete
- ▢ Stage skip
- ▨ Rob's text stage
- ■ On hold awaiting material

The chart tracks the progress of pages 001–224 across the stages: 1st draft text done, Edited text back, Images sourced, 1st layout done, Layouts to RV, Gone to repro.

remain, the extra few days are usually given without major issue. With reference to a point I made earlier, pay particular attention to those stages of a schedule that involve external suppliers, particularly if their contribution is vital to the ongoing progress of the project.

What's in the budget?

As well as time, all projects need to be financed. Make sure every key stage of the project is costed and adheres to the budget. Agree in advance all costs for external suppliers such as photographers or illustrators, and try to establish a flat fee for their part of the project rather than a flexible day rate. This provides much more control over the budget and ensures there won't be any nasty surprises on completion of the project. There's nothing wrong with a little negotiation at this stage, but do be realistic about paying appropriately for the skills of the suppliers. If you want to maintain a good working relationship with a trusted photographer, for example, don't expect them to continually accept budgetary cuts from one project to the next. ⊡

⬆ The chart above represents the progress of each page of this book during the writing, editing, image sourcing and/or creation, and layout stages of this book. It's created in InDesign for ease of use; no specialist software was needed. As you can see, I'm just about to complete this spread.

⊖ Considerations

WITH THOUGHT AND CREATIVITY

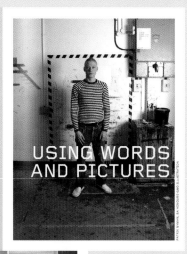

USING WORDS AND PICTURES

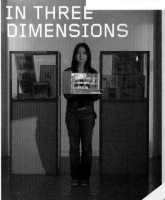

IN THREE DIMENSIONS

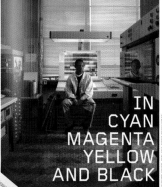

IN CYAN MAGENTA YELLOW AND BLACK

What have I forgotten?

With ever-greater experience, you're increasingly less likely to overlook key stages. However, it's always worth asking, "Are there any differences between this project and those that I've worked on in the past?" If so, what? It may be a specific type of illustration, or a print job using materials you're not familiar with. The panels opposite contain lists of possible points that you should consider when planning and scheduling a project. Use them as a prompt when planning your own workflow.

PROFILE
ES MEDCRAFT

The day after he completed his degree course, James started work at United Visual Artists where he had freelanced during the course. "I have been involved in producing graphics for U2 World Tour and MTV channel. Yesterday we finished a blue screen and today I'm adding dancing animations!"

James explained how the optional year's industrial attachment which he chose to take has been invaluable, not only to build up contacts but to gain confidence. He has worked with onedotzero, BskyB, RSA Films, Dazzle Films and John Brown Citrus Publications.

"On the typography pathway, we have learnt so much more than typeface recognition. We have been taught to think [ ] ideas. I design to communicate core ideas and [ ] to aid understanding. Concise unambiguous [ ] is at the heart of design".

[ ] exhibited in the Interact 1 exhibition [ ] ence, light 3000, started as an [ ] into the representation of sound [ ] der TM's cover of The Smiths [ ] Goes Out'. 'Light 3000 [ ] tion with past

◪ The 2006/2007 prospectus for the London College of Communication required strict adherence to the publishing schedule. A recent name change from the London College of Printing prompted the designers to explore the idea of communication and the ambitions of the students by using their portraits, all of which were art-directed by the designers.

Design: +Plus with photography by Joe Duggan

Generic planning considerations

➔ Have project-specific key stages been established?

➔ Has the client agreed in writing to the project's objectives?

➔ Are all the members of your team in possession of the appropriate skills for the project?

➔ Are there enough people allocated to the project?

➔ Are the work allocations appropriate, or have any team members been overloaded?

➔ Is there a proper network in place for communicating and recording project-specific information?

➔ Have all costs been placed against the budget?

➔ Are there any special requirements for specialist hardware or software that should be costed against the project?

➔ Have all the stages been built into the available schedule?

➔ Is there enough contingency built into the schedule?

➔ Has all the necessary photography and/or illustration been commissioned or sourced?

➔ Have all external suppliers agreed to, and committed to, the proposed schedule in writing?

Print-specific considerations

➔ Has someone placed repro and print?

➔ Has your printer agreed in writing to the delivery schedule?

➔ Have you allowed enough time for checking proofs and possible corrections?

➔ Does your client need time to check and approve proofs?

➔ Are you providing an extra set of proofs for your client, or should the printer deliver them directly?

➔ Will your printer organize the delivery of the printed project, or should that be organized separately?

➔ Will your printer store material and archive files in order to facilitate subsequent reprints, or will that be your responsibility?

Web-specific considerations

➔ Have the site structure and design style been approved by the client?

➔ Are you in possession of all the content needed to complete the project?

➔ Have web hosting and a domain been set up, and has the responsibility for actioning this key stage been agreed?

➔ Have the marketing and promotion of the new site been addressed and factored into the price?

➔ Has ultimate responsibility for the ongoing management of online content been agreed with the client?

➔ Is there provision in the budget for troubleshooting added content?

➔ A great deal of today's bulk printing is carried out in the Far East where costs are relatively low. However, this does of course mean a month or more must be added to the schedule to allow for shipping by sea. Air freight is much quicker of course, but is, in general, prohibitively expensive and would cancel any cost savings.

A typical print project workflow

This is based on the typical workflow required to design and produce a publication such as a brochure, an annual report, or an illustrated book. However, most print-based design projects will follow a broadly similar sequence to this example.

Establish the specific priorities and key stages of the project
based on the fullest possible brief from your client or creative director

Establish the schedule
keeping a close eye on all overlapping stages that may create bottlenecks

Establish clear lines of communication between team members
such as contact telephone numbers and e-mail addresses

Provide a clear brief for all team members
which may differ for those that are dealing with different areas of the project (e.g. designer and photographer)

Confirm the budget for all team members
splitting it down into its constituent parts as relevant

Appoint the printer
confirming all costs in writing as specified in the original budget

Obtain client's approval
of all design work

Send the project out for repro and print
after prepress checks of all design work and all images used

Establish the budget
*keeping the image budget separate
from other key areas such as freelance
design fees or print and repro*

**Seek client approval of
the project outline**
*if this was an agreed stage when you
were commissioned for the project*

Appoint your project team
*who may be in-house or freelance
depending on the project's needs*

**Confirm the schedule for
all team members**
*ensuring that it's clear where areas overlap,
and highlighting all interim deadlines*

**Commission all images
and illustrations**
*or confirm their availablility if they
are being supplied by a client*

Begin design work

Check color proofs
and make all necessary corrections

Check corrected color proofs
*and seek client's approval if required as
part of your commission*

Approve for press

A typical online project workflow

This is based on the usual workflow required to produce an online presence such as a website, web content management system or intranet project. Most web-related projects will generally follow a similar sequence of events.

Establish the client's key objectives for the project
and gather any relevant information from the team involved with development

Prepare a timeline and agree a schedule for development
ensuring that deadlines are set for the supply of specific content

Outsource any areas which you'd prefer not to handle
such as complex web development/ programming needed for database-driven projects

Set up the backend details,
allocating budget and staff to ensure that web hosting, domains and technical requirements are in place

Create the draft site
as a mock-up of the overall design and functionality, seeking approval from the client before proceeding further

Match content to the design
adapting material where necessary

Troubleshoot the website
prior to the site going live, both locally and on a testing server

Confirm a marketing strategy
deciding how the site will be promoted when it goes live

Prepare costings and ensure there is sufficient budget
for any overrun in technical areas and for content and sourced images

Appoint the project team,
deciding who will be team leader and who will work on each section of the project

Create a site map,
working with your client and the design team to agree on the content needed for the entire project

Start producing pages and content
while testing at regular intervals

Liaise with the client
ensuring the site is on schedule, with enough time for the editing and optimization of images and other external content

Liaise with any external team members
and set up regular meetings to ensure work matches the original brief

Put the site live
and carry out additional testing on a variety of platforms using an assortment of web browsers

Submit site to search engines
optimizing website visibility, and fine-tune any aspects of site functionality

Confirm ongoing maintenance
as websites aren't static and need regular updates

The professionals' view

Throughout this chapter we've discussed how to plan and schedule projects in order to avoid coming unstuck with your clients and your collaborators or colleagues. You've read my take on it, but how do other graphics professionals approach this important area of project and image management?

To find out, I asked a number of designers what, apart from ultimately meeting an agreed deadline, they considered to be the most important aspect of planning and scheduling a new project. It was clear from the answers given that a major priority for many designers lies in allowing enough time to analyze the brief properly.

"A number of criteria need to be met, but a key element in our planning process is to allow enough *creative time* in the schedule to ensure that we're able to properly consider the client's brief in order to produce the appropriate creative solution," says Peter Dawson of Grade. He adds, "Deadlines must be realistic in the first place, and they must be married to a budget that's appropriate for the

client's expectations and requirements." Russell Hrachovec of compoundEye agrees with this view when he says, "We always try to give ourselves time to gestate the project properly, developing the ideas we have in order to bounce them off the client and make changes if necessary." David Johnston of Accept and Proceed also endorses this viewpoint, stating, "I always try to ensure that the schedule allows for client buy-in and sign-off—it's no use hitting the deadline in time, only to find out that the client has changed their mind or doesn't like the solution."

Setting the available budget against chargeable studio time is also of paramount importance when planning a schedule. Ian Pape of Fonda puts this into perspective,

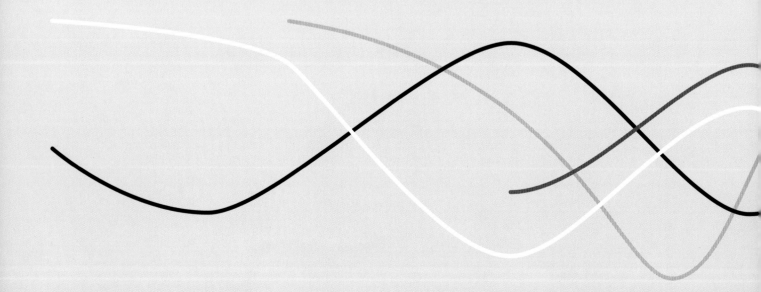

saying, "The best creative solution and how to achieve it is always at the forefront of our planning, along with keeping the client happy of course, but making a profit is also up there as a necessarily important consideration."

Unforeseeable circumstances also figure largely in designers' responses to scheduling issues. "If you're efficient when planning a project, the less stressful a project will be, and more time will be created along the way to help deal with those inevitable unforeseen circumstances," says Michel Vrána of Black Eye Design. It's not just unknown occurrences that can throw schedules out either—clients will often fail to take into account vital stages that they're not familiar with when looking toward their own perceived deadlines.

"The final artwork stage is sometimes overlooked by clients," say Sara and Patrick Morrissey of Forever Studio. "They tend to think that everything is *ready to go* as soon as they've approved a visual, without considering the time it takes to get a job ready for press or online publishing, so this should be allowed for."

Efficiency isn't the only thing that figures as an important consideration for designers. "Quality of life!" says Jonathan Kenyon of Vault 49. "Oppressive deadlines and too many late nights sap creativity and dull the senses. We owe it to ourselves and our clients to allow breathing space in and around projects, so we have time to experiment rather than just churning out tried and tested

formulas." Ultimately, of course, schedules are often at the mercy of the client's requirements, which can't be finitely predicted. Stefan Bucher of 344 Design sums it up perfectly when he says, "My fondest wish is to avoid colliding deadlines, but most of my clients move at their own speeds, regardless of any advance planning. All one can do is build in as much flexibility as possible. What makes my clients wonderful partners in crime also makes them ill suited to strict timetables."

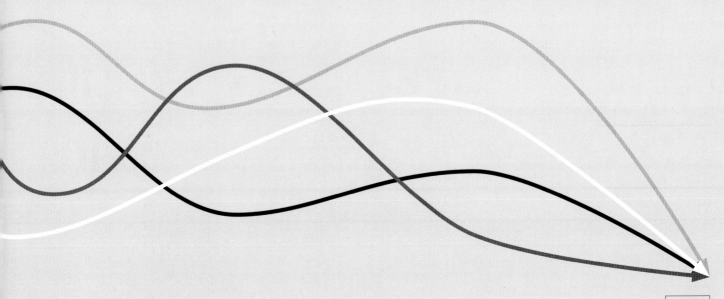

Sourcing, commissioning & working with suppliers

It's now possible to brief a photographer on the other side of the world by phone or e-mail and have high-resolution images on your desktop a few hours later. You can log on to an image library website and within minutes find just the image you were after, sometimes for only a few dollars. However, there's a certain individual quality to work that results from a good collaborative relationship between a designer and their suppliers. If you build strong ties with photographers, picture researchers, illustrators, and printers, you'll soon find that the benefits show through in the quality of your end results.

Supplier relationships

It's important to build and consistently add to a list of trusted suppliers across all areas in which you commission. Don't forget, the photographers, illustrators, and freelance designers that you use regularly help to provide the breadth of service that you're able to offer your clients. For this reason, working relationships with your regular suppliers should be considered as important as the working relationships you have with in-house colleagues.

Freelance photographers, illustrators & designers

There are people I always enjoy working with for all sorts of reasons, and with whom I continue to work as often as projects allow; but I'm also always on the lookout for people to add to the list. When you come across someone you've not worked with before, try to ascertain how suitable he or she is for the kind of projects you work on. If you think they may have the makings of a reliable supplier, begin by commissioning a "sample," such as providing photos for an internal presentation or working up some layout ideas for a project. This way, if things don't work out you'll have avoided jeopardizing an important project.

If, however, your new supplier made a good job of the initial commission, commit to further suitable projects. However, never stop assessing new suppliers. Look carefully at how reliable they continue to be over a longer period, and ensure that the quality of the work doesn't drop once they've made their first good impression. A true professional will deliver his or her best every time. ⊡

⬆ If you work with someone regularly, you can rely on them to provide their own creative input on projects. Photographer Simon Punter noticed the sunlight on the fence outside his studio when shooting these posters for RotoVision, and used it to good effect.
Design: Cyklon / Photography: Simon Punter

⬆ This series of, to date, five books published by
RotoVision have all been designed by the same freelance
designer. This has given the series a visual coherence
which would have been difficult to maintain under
different circumstances. The spreads shown are
from *Poster-Art*, by Charlotte Rivers.
Design: Laki 139

→ Supplier relationships

Pay close attention to their willingness to work to your budgets from one project to the next, but don't expect them to accept constant reductions in fees either. Assess how honest they are about their own workload when they commit to a project and a deadline. If a supplier agrees to a commission, it's up to him to meet that commitment regardless of any agreements he may have made with other clients. Monitor their willingness to accept direction from you. If they are consistently reluctant to allow you to input creatively to the project, the working relationship will break down quickly.

Repro houses & printers

Other vital suppliers include the repro houses and printers you use regularly. It's important to consider them as a part of the creative team too, as a good reprographic expert or design-led printer can add much to the final result. Some argue that the working relationships you form with print suppliers are less personal than those formed with individual freelancers, but personally I disagree. If you think of a printer as a large factory building with possibly hundreds of employees then it does seem impersonal, but essentially you are still dealing directly with one or two people as your main contacts, so

why should it be any different? On a practical level, reliability, quality, and a willingness to contribute creatively to your projects are obviously at the top of the list when it comes to buying print—and of course, they should be financially competitive. Printers will have set prices for specific types of work, which they use as a basis for quotations; but your favored print suppliers may be willing to discuss costs if they know you'll be placing a lot of work with them.

ISPs & hosting services

This doesn't have a whole lot to do with commissioning artwork, but it's relevant to

the supplier relationship discussion. Signing up to an ISP or purchasing web hosting services will involve contractual commitment, so spend time on your research. Ask around, read magazine reviews, and use the web to search for impartial views as opposed to advertising or targeted marketing campaigns. Clients may come to you with their hosting in place, which isn't always a good thing if it's not up to scratch, so if necessary suggest a switch, but be sure your advised option delivers what it promises. Hosting packages change all the time in terms of features and pricing, so always remain flexible. A good standard of readily available technical

⬆ It's likely that, at some point in your career, you'll be required to attend a "press pass" where you'll check running sheets for quality during a print run. It's important to maintain good working relationships with your regular printers if you are to make a success of this type of interaction with your suppliers.
Image: Star Standard Industries (Pte) Ltd.

support is also essential, especially if you're less used to working within an online environment. Finally, just as with printers, having a point of human contact can often help solve technical issues much more swiftly than wading through a mountain of online help pages, so always try to maintain good relationships with your main support contacts.

Maintaining the relationship

To maintain a good working relationship with a supplier, you need to invest in that relationship and build trust. For example, I always try to give a supplier a call (not send an e-mail) when I've received commissioned work in order to thank them. This isn't always practical because of time differences and so on, but it is the polite thing to do and I think it makes a difference to their perception of you as a client. If you always do your best to be both realistic and honest with your suppliers, they will usually reciprocate—if they don't, it's time to move on.

Briefing photographers & illustrators

All commissioned work begins with a brief, and the better the brief, the better the end result will be. A poorly constructed brief is the first sign that a project hasn't been thought through properly, and will reflect badly on your own abilities to commission work. This in turn will discourage suppliers from working with you, so it's really important to put the effort in and to be completely clear about what you require from the outset.

Photographers

When commissioning photography, and before contacting a photographer, draw up a shoot list that fulfils the project's requirements. This will help to indicate what can be achieved with the available budget, and enable you to focus on what may have to be dropped from your "ideal" image selection. The next thing I normally consider is whether or not I actually need to attend the whole shoot. For a complex and varied shoot it's essential that the photographer is provided with some on-site art direction— at least on the first day or so—or there's no recourse for you if you're not happy with the final results. However, simple photography that doesn't require lots of art direction is a different matter. It may be that you want to photograph a number of similar items with a consistent lighting arrangement. In this situation you probably need not attend, and can arrange to approve a couple of test shots e-mailed to you as low-resolution JPEGs before the shoot goes ahead.

Similarly, the way you brief photographers can vary enormously. If you're attending the shoot you can discuss each shot at length and in person, and the creative brief becomes largely verbal. If, however, you're not in attendance, it's important to provide a detailed written brief (as well as having a general conversation about the shoot before it commences). A written brief provides you with recourse should things go wrong. In the brief you should be clear about your views on the style of the photography you're commissioning; so agree on lighting, styling, backdrops, models, locations, props, and so on. If you don't, the photographer will make his or her own decisions on the day, which may or may not be what you had in mind.

◄ This image of *AURA* magazine was shot along with a number of other pieces for inclusion in a RotoVision book, *Mag-Art*. A carefully prepared brief for the photographer outlining our general requirements meant that it wasn't necessary for me to be at the shoot for its entire duration. All images were approved as e-mailed low-resolution JPEGs.
Design: LAKI 139

It's also important to discuss how the images are going to be used, as the photographer will make some key decisions based on this information. Here are some typical points to consider specifying as part of your brief—some are technical and some more creative:

Digital or film

There are still some distinct advantages with film. Large-format film cameras produce originals that can be scanned at resolutions capable of producing much larger images than digital equipment—although ever-larger-resolution digital camera backs are in production.

Resolution

If shooting digitally, the camera's sensor resolution and the file-size settings will govern the size of the printed image, so speak to the photographer about scaling issues. Of course, if the photos are for online use only this is less of an issue.

Orientation, proportion & background

If an image is intended for use as a full-bleed image on one page of a magazine, it should be in portrait format with enough bleed area around the main subject to allow the image to be cropped without significant compromise. If it's to be used across a spread of the same magazine, it should be landscape, with the same considerations for bleed and crop. If the image is to be a "cutout" it should be shot against a white, or possibly blue, background to make accurate construction of a clipping path easier.

Empty areas

This sounds like a curious consideration, but if an image is intended for use as a cover shot for a brochure or magazine, there will need to be clean, visually uncluttered areas for placement of the masthead and other typographic elements.

Simultaneous RAW & JPEG shooting

Many digital cameras can be set to produce a RAW file with an accompanying JPEG file which can be supplied immediately as a means of editing and selecting your final choice of images from a shoot. The JPEGs can also be used as "positionals" in layouts while the RAW files are undergoing post-production work.

Post-production work

Unless you ask them not to, your photographer will process the RAW image files before supplying them, but the brief should specify any additional work that you require beyond the normal color balancing, sharpening, and artifact removal. Think carefully about how much post-production work you want the photographer to do, as there will be a cost implication. ➔

➔ This cover shot for *LEMON*, published by the team behind *GUM* magazine, is a great example of how clear space can be incorporated into a shot and used for the placement of a masthead.
Design: Kevin Grady / Colin Metcalf (GUM)

→ Briefing photographers & illustrators

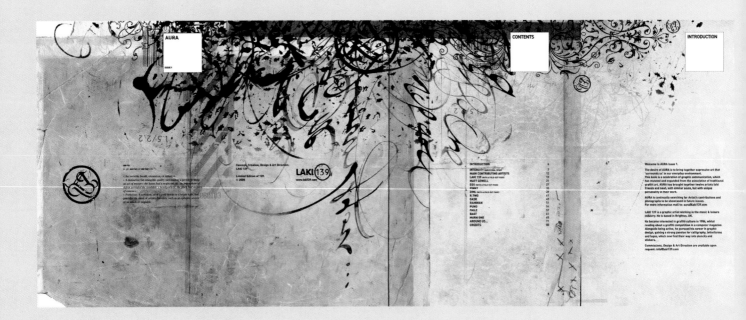

Budget, schedule & responsibilities

Always be clear and realistic with a photographer when discussing budget and schedule. Run through the shoot list and agree the number of shots, taking into account any necessary props and materials, who will source them, and who pay for them. Make sure the photographer is not planning to hire any specialist equipment that will incur additional costs before discussing it with you. Talk about any model requirements, who pays the models, and who is responsible for model-release forms. Find out how many shots the photographers think they can do per day and compare this to both the available time and the budget, if you are basing that on an agreed day rate. I prefer to settle on a flat fee before any photography begins, but you do have to be honest about the amount of work and negotiate additional costs if things don't go according to plan.

Illustrators

The principles behind forming a brief for a photographer also apply here, but there are one or two issues that are peculiar to commissioning illustrations. Style, budget, and schedule are of course common considerations, but while a photographer who may have a favorite personal style can usually adapt to a brief through the use of different equipment or lighting set-ups, this is not often the case with an illustrator. Most will have one or maybe two distinctive illustrative styles that they generally stick to, so the choice of who to use is governed more closely by this factor. This isn't true of all illustrators, of course, but it's generally the case. Remember that you may be working with someone who is located in another country or time zone, which complicates verbal communication, and makes it all the more important to get the written brief right.

Make sure you know what materials the illustrator plans to use, and specify this as part of the brief. If the finished piece requires scanning on a drum scanner, for example, the paper or board must be flexible enough

⬆ The highly distinctive style of calligraphic illustration used in *AURA*, a self-published fanzine celebrating graffiti art, is actually the result of a well-considered brief from the designer to himself. The ability to fulfill one's own creative brief is as important as honing your ability to brief others.
Design: Laki 139

to wrap around the drum. The alternative is an additional stage of photography, which will take time and add cost. Talk about scale too, and decide what percentage enlargement the illustrator should work to in relation to the size at which the piece will be reproduced. Make sure you check the maximum size your repro house can scan, and pass this information on in the brief.

Many illustrators now work digitally, but a number of the older rules still apply. For example, if a piece of technical line artwork is to be produced "twice up" (200% of the size at which it will print), decide on the line weight you require and brief the illustrator to use double this line weight on the original. If the illustration is supplied as a vector artwork (see pages 130–131) scale is less of an issue, but if it is a rasterized image, you must be clear about the size at which the image will be published to avoid resolution problems.

Preparing contracts

Before you start any work with a photographer or illustrator, it's essential that you exchange some form of contract with them. This should at the very least include the agreed fee, deadlines, and payment terms to be adhered to when they supply you with their invoice. Contracts for relatively straightforward projects don't have to be complex documents with pages of legalese to wade through. They can take the simple form of a purchase order which specifies the key targets and budget, and can also include an outline of the brief which reiterates what you require.

One thing that must be clarified, however, is who owns the copyright of any images produced. The fact that you've paid for the work doesn't necessarily mean that you own it outright, so make sure you take this into account for all commissioned work. You must also indemnify yourself against any potential problems that may arise from your suppliers infringing the copyright of a third party, so include a clause that covers this area in your small print.

➡ I use this simple form as both a purchase order and a contract when I commission any creative work for RotoVision. It covers all the key areas that require clarification, and prevents any misunderstandings about what's required. If necessary, a more detailed brief can be attached as a separate sheet.

TIP
If you can find an example of the style of photography or illustration that you want, include it as part of the brief. This will be of enormous help when explaining what you require from the brief, bearing in mind that you're talking to another visual person.

037

Copyright

Put simply, copyright is defined as an exclusive set of rights granted to regulate the use of a specific expression of an idea or work, and may prevail in a wide range of creative and intellectual forms. Although copyright laws vary from country to country, in practice copyright generally exists to protect a person's rights over his or her own work, and to prevent that work being used by others without permission.

Contrary to popular belief, copyright doesn't have to be registered officially. It is in fact automatic as long as the work exists in physical form. You can't copyright an idea that's not recorded in some way, and in most cases it's limited to a specific period of time as dictated by local copyright law. In most countries this is 70 years after the death of the person who originally created the work—although this can vary and should be checked. Copyright law only covers the particular form in which the idea has been recorded, not the concept behind the original idea or the technique used to produce the work. An example of this would be a photographer taking a picture of a famous landmark, such as the Statue of Liberty. The photographer's image would be copyright, and could only be reproduced with the photographer's permission; but that doesn't stop other photographers shooting more images of "Liberty Enlightening the World" from exactly the same spot.

Images & copyright

As a designer you must be clear about what you can and can't use in the creation of your project. The bottom line is that without the copyright holder's permission you cannot use their copyright-protected material in any way. The issue is particularly relevant to images, especially now that the Internet has made the electronic distribution of material so easy. Always seek permission to use an image and make sure you get that permission in writing. Be clear about the license that is being granted if you are purchasing the rights to an image from a photographer or stock photo library (see pages 042–045), and check whether a written credit is required as part of the grant of use. Check whether there are clauses that restrict the image's use in certain countries, or for certain types of business that may be against the copyright owner's principles. This process may not always involve a fee, but be aware that free images are still protected by copyright law and still require permission, under the terms by which they were legally acquired, if they're to be used commercially.

If you're creating material as part of a commission, make sure that it's clear who will own the copyright over that work. If you're an employee it's most likely that your contract of employment states that the copyright belongs to your employer. However, if you're working as a freelance give some thought to whether or not you are prepared to sign over the copyright for anything you create. It may be worth more to you to retain copyright with whatever conditions you have to take on board. For example, many designers and illustrators will retain copyright of any artwork they produce, only giving the commissioning employer the right to use the work once for the purpose specified in the brief. If the piece is required for an alternative use an additional fee will then have to be negotiated. ⮕

◤ ⬆ ⮕ All these images are of the same physical object, but neither photographer can exercise any right over the other, even if the images had been shot from almost exactly the same position and angle like the images above and to the right.

Images: iStockphoto.com

→ Copyright

Creative Commons

Copyright is often accompanied with the phrase "All Rights Reserved." This means that, in effect, the material cannot be used under any circumstances without prior written agreement from the copyright holder (or an agent with power to grant a license). While this offers umbrella protection to the copyright holder and their work, many people argue that this form of copyright is too restrictive. For example, many people are happy for their work to be used for non-profit-making and/or educational projects free of charge, as long as the work is credited to them. The relatively new idea of Creative Commons is intended to offer a middle ground to cover such cases. Creative Commons was formed by a group of like-minded experts in 2001 and offers a range of alternatives that provide "Some Rights Reserved" copyright as opposed to the "All Rights Reserved" of traditional copyright. It enables people who want to share their work in specific ways to do so more easily without losing the ownership and rights of the original piece. The collaborative way in which many websites have been able to develop is due in part to the existence of Creative Commons. For example, just over 25 million images on the extremely successful image-sharing website Flickr (www.flickr.com) use CC licenses.

It's important to note that Creative Commons licenses are irreversible, so think carefully before applying such a license to a piece of work that you may want to offer someone exclusively at a later date.

⬆ A Creative Commons license enables people who want to share their work in specific ways to do so more easily without losing the ownership and rights of the original piece, where "some rights" rather than "all rights" are reserved.

The six main Creative Commons licenses

Here's a brief explanation of the options provided by the six most commonly used Creative Commons licenses. The correct combinations of Creative Commons icons representing these options are shown at the bottom of the page. For further information on exactly what the licenses are and how they work in your particular territory, refer to the Creative Commons website at www.creativecommons.org.

1. Attribution allows others to distribute and build upon your original work, including for commercial purposes, as long as you are credited for the original creation. This allows the most in terms of what others can do with your work.

2. Attribution Share Alike allows others to distribute and build upon your original work, including for commercial purposes, as long as you are credited and they license their new work under identical terms. All derivatives will also allow commercial use.

3. Attribution No Derivatives allows others to redistribute your work commercially and non-commercially as long as the work remains completely unchanged and is credited to you.

4. Attribution Non-commercial allows others to build upon your work and distribute for non-commercial use. Their new work must credit you and be non-commercial, but it doesn't have to be licensed under identical terms.

5. Attribution Non-commercial Share Alike allows others to build upon your work and distribute non-commercially as long as you are credited and they license their new work under identical terms. All derivatives will be non-commercial.

6. Attribution Non-commercial No Derivatives allows others to download and share your work as long as you are fully credited, but the work can't be changed in any way or used commercially. The original work must also be linked back to you. This allows the least in terms of what others can do with your work.

1

4

2

5

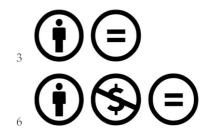

3

6

Using image libraries

Image libraries, or stock photography agencies to give them another name, have existed for many years. The first such libraries date as far back as the 1920s, when they carried photographic stock composed largely of unselected shots, known as "overs," from commercial magazine commissions. By the 1980s the successful libraries had expanded into a serious resource business for many designers, with photographers shooting material specifically for the libraries.

The 1990s saw many of the smaller libraries combining to form much larger companies such as Getty Images and Corbis, and the advent of the Internet and instant online purchasing consolidated the position of image libraries within today's creative image workflow. The ability to download free "comp" or low-resolution images for use in mock-up visuals before committing to a purchase allows for valuable creative options; furthermore, many of the bigger libraries now also carry large collections of traditional illustration in addition to photographic material. The relatively new

"microstock" libraries, which sell exclusively online and offer images for as little as $1.00, have added yet another choice of available image sources.

All this choice and value is great for designers, but it raises a couple of points that should be taken into consideration when sourcing images. The first and possibly most important question to ask yourself is whether or not you would benefit from commissioning a photographer or illustrator. Image libraries are generally quicker and more cost effective, but think about the alternatives—an image specially shot for

➲ Getty Images has an enormous range of material to offer for purchase as rights-managed or royalty-free, plus their new rights-managed licence (see panel on page 043). Their website is well designed and easy to use, and features a fully customizable search facility to narrow down your choices.
http://creative.gettyimages.com

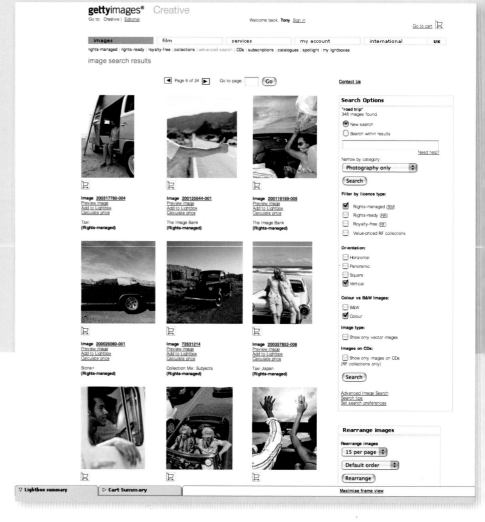

your project could add value and quality. However, bear in mind that high-quality image libraries such as Getty Images (see below) are also able to provide unique rights-managed material to match a brief.

Rights-managed images

Images sold on a rights-managed or "rights-protected" basis are subject to restrictions in their use, based on the fee negotiated with the image library, which will generally involve working with an account handler. If the image is to be used for a print project, for example, you'll have to inform the library of

the size at which the image will be reproduced, such as half-page or full-bleed across a spread. Similarly, you'll need to inform the library if you're producing different versions of a publication, say in different languages, for distribution worldwide—there will usually be a fee levied for each language edition, in which case you may want to consider purchasing "world language rights." Finally, print quantities will also be required before a price is agreed.

You can also negotiate exclusive rights to publish your chosen images, sometimes over a specific period of time, which will add to the cost but may be extremely important in the case of high-profile projects. Imagine the scenario of two major companies, operating in the same area of business, publishing annual reports with the same image on the cover. Purchasing from a rights-managed source will enable you to avoid the chances of this happening.

Royalty-free images

None of the above restrictions apply to royalty-free images, which can be purchased online or as collections of similar subjects or themes on CD and DVD. For a one-off payment, images purchased in this way can be used as many times and in as many ways as required. Do check the small print, as ⊟

Rights-ready

This is a new type of license introduced by Getty Images. It's designed to simplify the purchase of high-quality images of a caliber normally associated with rights-managed material, by offering flat-rate pricing for specific categories such as print ad, book cover, web, and so on. You don't need to obtain a quotation based on image size, placement, or geographical rights. I think this will prove to be a popular option, particularly for editorial uses, and that other libraries may begin to offer similar terms in the future. Find out more at http://creative.gettyimages.com.

⬆ Registered users of the Getty Image website can set up virtual lightboxes, add notes, sort the stacking order, and even e-mail the lightbox to other members of their creative team.
http://creative.gettyimages.com

⊕ Using image libraries

there are occasionally some clauses that restrict the images' use, but generally they are yours to do with what you will. The price is usually based on their resolution or dimensions, governing how large they can be reproduced. This is particularly the case with microstock libraries that, for example, offer a 72ppi version of an image (for website use) for around $2.00, with larger 300ppi files from around $6.00 up to $15.00. Some sites also offer annual fee terms for a given number of daily downloads. Always be aware of the non-exclusivity of royalty-free images—the best images on any one site are the prime candidates for multiple purchases.

Always look to see how many have already been bought; the better sites provide a count of how many have been downloaded.

There's no doubt that without image libraries most designers' image requirements would be more complicated to source and maintain. However, it would be very short-sighted of a designer to assume that image libraries can provide all of their image needs, so make sure you maintain cordial links with your favored photographers and illustrators— you *will* need them.

TIP

If you're buying from a library that offers a variety of image sizes for download, consider buying the largest size possible, even if it's larger than your immediate needs. The image will be yours to use again for other projects if you wish, and you may need to use it at a larger size next time. It could be worth it for the sake of just a few dollars.

➡ This picture from the iStockphoto image library is offered at four sizes and/or resolutions and at a range of corresponding prices. The four options are all reproduced here at 300ppi to provide a visual comparison.

www.istockphoto.com

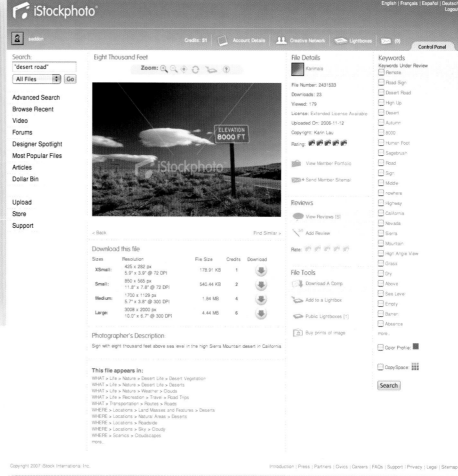

The professionals' view

To find out how other graphics professionals approach the everyday task of sourcing and commissioning images, and to see how working relationships are maintained, I asked what motivates their choice of who to work with. I also asked what lengths they go to in order to maintain good working relationships with the people they like to work with most.

"Trust is the most important motivation by far for us," says Paul Burgess of Loewy. "Photographers don't really pitch for commissions. Their previous work for either ourselves or other agencies is what brings them to our attention. Rapport and respect is crucial too—you need to get along. Overly opinionated photographers can be very hard to work with, and meek characters with little presence can be just as problematic." He goes on to say, "I believe in treating clients and suppliers just the same. We're all people that want to enjoy our time at work, so when we get on and respect one another it all works out." Peter Dawson of Grade backs up this viewpoint when he says, "I've had some great experiences working with many good

individual photographers and illustrators, and as a result dislike commissioning via agents or print buyers. You have to be able to work with the actual person as it's their work combined with their character, that's foremost in the selection process. You don't need prima donnas throwing a fit when a shoot runs over by 10 minutes!"

The appropriateness of an individual's working style is, of course, also at the forefront of the process. Personally, I never choose to work with someone purely on the basis of their availability—it's better to wait for them to become available if possible, or to keep looking. "There's always a risk when commissioning someone new, but style of work is so important and the creative style

has to be right for the job," says Ian Pape of Fonda. He also has an interesting point to make when it comes to maintaining cordial working relationships with Fonda's suppliers. "We don't do anything specific, we just try to be professional, hardworking and friendly with everyone we do business with. We do try to avoid the pub, however, particularly with suppliers we don't know so well."

I was also keen to find out what others saw as the most important considerations when briefing work to a photographer or illustrator. The consistent response from everyone I spoke to was, of course, clear and constant communication between all the individuals involved in a project. "Communication is the key," for Sara and Patrick Morrissey of Forever Studio. "They have to be briefed clearly, with emphasis on what the final solution should communicate, and to what audience." They add to this, "It's also vital that the creative people you work with are given the chance to input their ideas at the early stages of a project. This often results in more interesting and challenging creative work." David Johnston of Accept and Proceed agrees with this point when he says, "Make sure they're clear about the brief, but don't inhibit their creativity with too many constraints, as you never know what they may bring to the table." Ian Pape also raises a highly relevant point when he says, "We want to get the result that's right for the job, and can't afford to massage egos as part of this process. Therefore, the brief must clearly state what we want, when we need it and how much we are prepared to pay. At the same time, photographers and illustrators must still be allowed their own creative input."

Cataloging, processing & filing

This chapter discusses issues that are often quite technical in nature. As designers we are, first and foremost, creative people whose job it is to think about ideas. You may feel that all this technical stuff just gets in the way of free-flowing creativity, and that it's best left for someone else to deal with. To a certain extent I agree with you. However, in recent years our industry has irrevocably changed, and many of us are now required to be technical wizards as well as designers. The trick is to learn how to incorporate the technical stuff into your creative workflow in a way that enhances the whole process rather than turning it all into one big chore. If you've a full understanding of how images should be handled, the creative process is improved. And remember, the professional repro and print people haven't gone away; they're still there doing what they've always done. They can do a lot of this stuff for you, but it'll help you to get what you want if you can speak their language.

Hardware basics

Most of you are likely to already have some hardware in place, with either a Mac or a Windows PC fronting your system. If this is the case, your main considerations will center on which peripherals you need, such as monitors, scanners, printers, CD/DVD burners, and additional hard drives (strictly, hard disks) for extra storage and backup.

If, however, you're considering a fresh start or plan to upgrade your whole system, including the main workstation, my advice is to buy the best specification that you can possibly afford. My father, an engineer, always advised me never to buy a cheap wrench, as it would let me down at a crucial moment and I would regret the purchase. He was right (unfortunately I had to make the mistake of not following his advice in order to find out), and in many respects the same rule applies to computers. Build quality and the highest specification possible will reward you in the long term. This approach may sound indulgent, but quality isn't a luxury when applied to hardware that's integral to your business.

Capacity

With regard to hard-disk capacity, size actually does matter. The more free space available, the faster your workstation will run; and no matter how big the disk, you'll manage to fill it eventually. Image file sizes are increasing with every new generation of digital camera and with the more widespread use of files with higher bit depth—in order to keep up, hard disk capacities must grow.

A portable hard disk with a high capacity is a great addition to any hardware setup. It's an excellent option for transferring large amounts of data between locations or off-network workstations, and can be utilized as a secondary scratch disk (see Glossary), improving the performance of your computer. More importantly, portable hard disks provide you with the means to create a daily backup of all your current work, which can then be carried with you "off-site." Backups are covered in greater detail on pages 132–133.

Monitors

A good-quality screen is essential for all image work. LCD technology has improved considerably since the first flat screens appeared on the market, and they are now a viable alternative to the CRT (cathode-ray tube) monitor for image professionals. CRT monitors currently offer greater accuracy when it comes to high-end color work, but for all except the most color-critical workflows a flat screen is perfectly acceptable.

⊕ High-capacity portable hard drives, like this one from LaCie, are a great addition to your hardware setup. This particular product can store up to 320GB of data. Make sure the connections included both Firewire and USB 2.0 to maximize the number of workstations you can use the device with.

Image: LaCie

TIP

An external CD/DVD burner is the most flexible option when offered the choice between internal and external drives. If your chosen workstation is available with a range of build options, go for a basic internal reader and purchase a good-quality external disc burner as an extra. This can save money if you shop around, and if the drive develops a problem you can simply unplug it and get it fixed, or replace it without having to send your entire workstation out for repairs that could take weeks to complete.

TIP

Assess your physical workspace before you purchase any new hardware. Bulky equipment may not fit comfortably into the available space, and your working environment is extremely important if you spend a lot of time at your desk.

◩ Flat-screen technology has improved considerably over the last few years, making it viable for all but the most color-critical work.

Image: My Poor Brain / LaCie

What is creative asset management?

You're thinking that this sounds very technical and complicated, right? Well, I thought exactly the same thing when I was first introduced to the concept of digital asset management (DAM)—or creative asset management, as it is often called. I had always tried to stay organized when it came to managing complex design projects with a large number of images, and creative asset management sounded like it was going to make things more complicated; but I was wrong.

Creative asset management is not easy to define in a single sentence, as it can mean a lot of things. In the context of graphic design and image workflow it means acquiring, naming, filing, editing, processing, importing, despatching, and archiving. This sums up the processes that an average image would undergo during the course of a creative design project for either print or the web. The very act of downloading an image from a picture library and filing it on your workstation or a server before importing it into a layout is in effect creative asset management—but if it's neither planned nor controlled it's probably not *good* creative

asset management. In theory you should be able to refer back to that image at any point during the project and know where it came from, how much it cost, where it was intended to be used, what usage had been cleared, and so on. All the images that you acquire, regardless of their individual cost, collectively represent an investment in both money and time, so should be handled securely and with care. It's not just financial cost either—images can be of great value for personal or sentimental reasons, and should be looked after as carefully as other valued possessions. Creative asset management extends beyond the workplace, now that

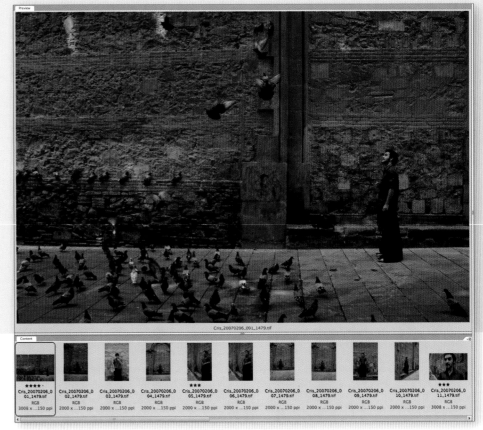

➔ Adobe Bridge is an excellent starting point for a typical creative asset management workflow.

Photography: Jason Keith

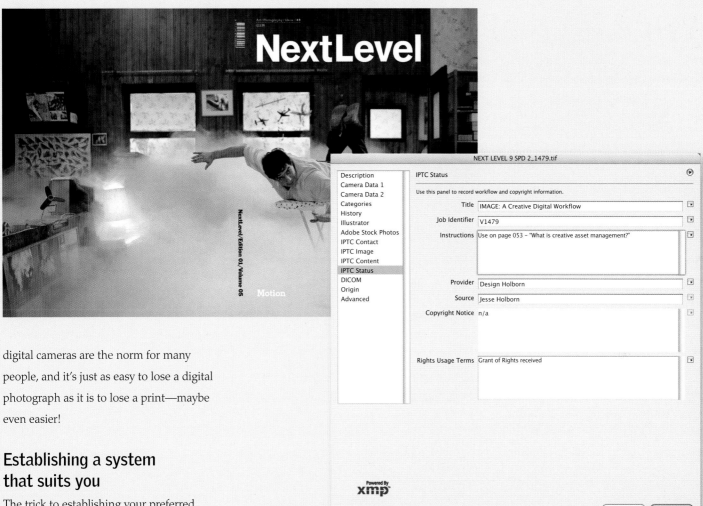

digital cameras are the norm for many people, and it's just as easy to lose a digital photograph as it is to lose a print—maybe even easier!

Establishing a system that suits you

The trick to establishing your preferred methods for creative asset management is to analyze your existing way of organizing material. The fact that you haven't implemented a planned system doesn't necessarily mean that you aren't already practicing creative asset management in some form—it might be that you simply haven't realized yet. Look at the procedures that you currently follow when editing and processing images, and decide if there's anything that can be built upon and

expanded. Be prepared to banish old habits if necessary, as these could undermine a new workflow and may be superseded by new technology that you adopt. There's also a good chance that your self-taught techniques, while working for you, won't fit with other industry-standard procedures, thus preventing efficient collaborative working within a creative team. ▣

⬆ A good creative digital workflow should allow information about an image to be accessed at any point during the design process. For example, the XMP panel shown above is common to all components of Adobe's Creative Suite and allows an image's embedded metadata (see pages 062–065) to be accessed quickly and easily.

Design: Design Holborn

⊕ What is creative asset management?

The average system for creative asset management will likely be composed of a standardized set of stages. First you should decide on a naming convention for all your image files, paying particular attention to whether or not it will work consistently for all the different types of project that you are likely to encounter. Second, once you have your material renamed and organized into a structured system of folders you should assess what happens to your images during the processing, cataloging, and end-use stages prior to printing or uploading to a website. Finally, you should look at how and where your images will be filed and stored, and decide which equipment and tools are required for that purpose. Backing up is extremely important, and, bizarrely, is often overlooked as a secondary consideration until the worst happens and important material is lost—at which point, of course, it's too late to act. Backup procedures are covered in more detail later in this chapter (see pages 132–133). Put simply, your creative asset management system should detail how to name, catalog, and process files, utilize them as required, and finally store them securely for future use.

Be as systematic as you can when putting your system together, and don't be tempted to tack catalogs created with new systems onto older existing catalogs. I can tell you from experience that it doesn't work well. Be consistent with all of the conventions that you come up with, particularly when it comes to naming and metadata entries (see pages 058–065). Do all you can to keep up with information about developing technologies that can help you to improve your system and allow you to cope with the inevitable demands of larger image sizes and the growth of your stored material. A word of caution too at this point: don't over-engineer your system and make it more complicated than it needs to be or it'll take over and cancel out the efficiencies it creates. Concentrate on the fundamentally important stages, and only add parts to your system if they are providing a genuine benefit.

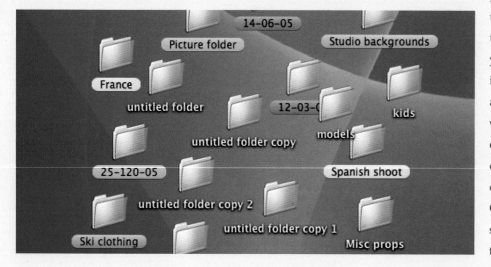

⬆ This screen shot of a chaotic desktop is shamelessly intended to make those of you whose desktops look like this feel guilty. This is definitely not the way to practice good creative asset management.

➡ When faced with the task of managing large volumes of images from one or more photo shoots, an effective creative asset management system will pay dividends.
Photography: Jason Keith

A creative asset management system

The following pages take you through the complete process by which you can assess and select images and create detailed catalogs at the same time. It may be possible within your own workflow to skip some of these stages—for example, you may eschew Bridge and go straight to the catalog stage. The information you'll need to make formative decisions can be found throughout the rest of this chapter.

Import a project's images to your workstation
either from a camera, or as a download from an image library, or from a supplied CD or DVD

Manually

Via software to rename files and add basic metadata

Backup all the original material to external drive or CD/DVD

Review all images fully using Bridge and add basic metadata
See pages 062–065 and 072–075

Use metadata templates wherever possible

Add star ratings to your top image choices

Use your catalog to create contact sheets for reference
or for distribution to other members of the creative team. See pages 078–079

A "List view" printout is useful for checking images against artwork

A JPEG version of a contact sheet is perfect for use as an e-mail attachment

Review the complete image set to ensure you have all the material you require
using a browser such as Bridge or, if you prefer, manually with your image-editing software

Organize the material using a stuctured system of folders

Rename your image files based on a standardized system and convert them to an appropriate format
See pages 058–061 and 073

Utilize Bridge to speed up the processing of any RAW files

Take advantage of Photoshop's batch-processing capabilities

Build your catalog using software such as Microsoft Expression Media or Extensis Portfolio
or import your images directly to a catalog if you've chosen to skip the Bridge stage. See pages 076–077

Add all extra metadata as required
based on a default arrangement of fields in your chosen software. See pages 076–077

Create catalog sets to help isolate image subdivisions within large catalogs
such as separate chapters of a book or individual web pages. See pages 076–077

Create an online gallery which can be accessed easily by all team members
and by your clients, if you wish to give them a preview of commissioned material. See pages 078–079

Process and adjust all images that have made the final selection for the project
See pages 100–129

Begin layouts

Preparing your files

Now that you understand more about what creative asset management entails, let's look in more detail at the techniques that should be employed when first preparing files for a catalog of images. As always, there are particular considerations that can be singled out for discussion.

What's in a name?

An intelligent approach to file naming is invaluable to an image-management workflow. To begin, it's generally a good idea to assign a unique code to each of your projects. Keep the coding short and simple, and incorporate it into the name of each image file for that project. This provides an instant visual link between image and project that doesn't require any asset-management software. Incidentally, this code can be assigned to all files for a project, not just

image files, and is useful for accounting and invoicing too, particularly if you combine it with a code for each of your clients. In addition, I always save images with appended file extensions (set in Photoshop's File Handling preferences), as it's useful to be able to identify file types without having to open them.

I prefer to include a unique and short (preferably one-word) description of an image file name, along with any other project or client codes. Some designers prefer to

beach_06_20060709_C12_1479.tif

📷 An example of a typical file name using the methods described. One can instantly see that the file is the sixth image of a beach photographed on the 9th July 2006, that the client code is C12, that it is linked to project number 1479, and that the image is formatted as a TIFF. If dates are not important, longer descriptions can be used. All this is achieved with just 30 characters.

Photography: Tony Seddon

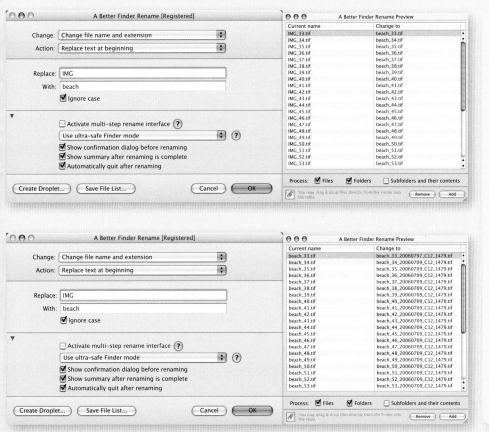

Batch renaming

Browsers and cataloging software all have batch-renaming capabilities, but for serious data management, I would highly recommend a specialist renaming package. There are several good packages available. A Better Finder Rename (shown left) is available for both Mac OSX and Windows from publicspace.net/ABetterFinderRename/index.html. The software provides an extensive range of options for renaming files of all kinds, potentially saving hours of monotonous clicking.

stick with the code that the camera (or photographer/image library) has already assigned to the image, or to devise their own system of coding that ties in with their storage and archiving system. This can work, but if you're looking for an image of a beach it's easier to look for "beach" than it is to remember that the beach picture is called, for example, IMG_6435.jpg. Images may, of course, have a description or keywords embedded in metadata, but you can't rely on this. Always put the description at the front of the file name, as this will enable you to go straight to it in a folder list by typing the first

few letters. If you've got more than one beach picture in the project, give each beach image a number, making its name unique within the project. Remember that the project code we talked about earlier will make these beach images unique from any beach images that you may have used in other, differently coded projects.

It's sometimes useful to include a date in the image name, particularly if you need to track when you received or purchased it, but use the order year/month/day if you want the files to appear in date order when sorted in an alphabetical list. ⊡

⬆ A simple two-stage renaming procedure using A Better Finder Rename produces a managed set of images from a series of ambiguously named files.

⊙ Preparing your files

Permissible characters

⊇ Cross-platform compatibility for your files relies on the use of permissible characters only when naming images or other documents. Limiting yourself to the following is the safest option for maximum portability.

0–9	(all numbers)
A–Z	(all uppercase letters)
a–z	(all lowercase letters)
_	underscore
-	hyphen
.	period

⊇ File names should never begin or end with a period.
⊇ Never use more than one period in a file name, and limit its use to separating the main part of the file name from the last three characters, which make up the file extension.
⊇ Blank spaces can be used, but it's best to avoid them in practice and use an underscore instead. This is particularly relevant if a file is being transferred via the web or posted to a website.

Avoid using prohibited characters (see panel left), as these are reserved for specific functions in either the Mac OSX or Windows operating systems. Finally, give some consideration to the number of characters used in the name. Mac OSX and Windows file names can comprise up to 255 characters, but older systems only accept a maximum of 31 characters, so if you need to share your files with others, check their setup and act accordingly. To be honest, 31 characters is usually enough, and I find very long file names rather unwieldy, so it's not a bad convention to stick to on the whole.

The digital filing cabinet

Before you begin the cataloging process, give one more thought to the way that you've organized your original files and folders on your workstation or server. Good filing practice is fundamental to all creative asset management, regardless of any subsequent cataloging activity—so devise a consistent and accessible method for structuring your folders. Again, my advice is to keep it simple. Avoid lots of nested folders that could make locating your material difficult. Utilize parts of the naming convention that we've just discussed, such as the project code, and stick

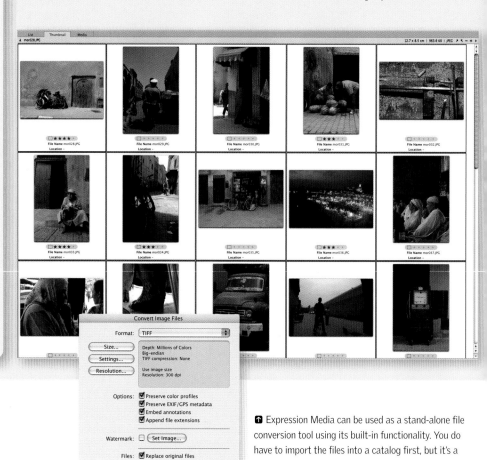

↥ Expression Media can be used as a stand-alone file conversion tool using its built-in functionality. You do have to import the files into a catalog first, but it's a quick way of converting files to an alternative format.

to clear and concise folder names. Your cataloging software will of course direct you straight to a selected file if the links have been maintained, but well-organized folders are essential. My recommendation is to keep separate projects together in their own clearly labeled folders, along with all the relevant material. This ensures archiving is kept simple when a project is complete, and any images associated with a project can be located quickly without trawling through an enormous digital archive. Remember that you can always keep additional copies of images that are reused often on your workstation for quick access, but make sure you include those files as part of your final archive when the project is stored.

Converting image formats

Now is a good point in your workflow to carry out any necessary file-format changes. For an overview of format properties, refer to pages 094–095 and to the Glossary at the end of the book. It's a good idea at this point to liaise with relevant suppliers to ascertain which formats they prefer. Photoshop is very workflow-friendly, so use the built-in automation or custom Actions to convert image files from one format to another. Also, Expression Media can be used as a stand-alone batch conversion tool.

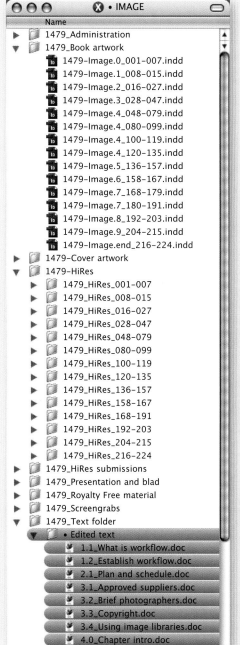

A word of caution

Make sure the system you adopt is fully expandable and adaptable. For example, what happens if a client you've worked with for years suddenly changes its name because another partner has joined? If images are named for the client, do you go back and update your entire archive with the new name, or do you continue with something different? If the client had first been assigned a code, it doesn't matter how many times the name is changed. Simplicity helps the backup procedure too, and makes it easier to check that your filing structure is completely up to date.

⬆ For large projects—like this book for example—set up folders for all your images which correspond to the page range of each layout file. It's not necessarily the default way but it does work well. Keep things simple and avoid too many nested folders that require lots of downward navigation.

What is metadata?

The term "metadata" is now universally accepted and easily defined—it is data about data. But what does it mean in reality? Well, it means that by accessing an image's metadata you can find out pretty much anything you want about that image—including when it was taken, where it came from, and in some cases who owns the copyright.

Much of the metadata that a file automatically carries with it will be mainly of interest to photographers, but there's a lot of recorded information that's incredibly useful for graphic designers too, if you know how to tap into it and use it to your advantage.

Types of metadata

Let's have a look at some of the types of metadata found embedded in images. First there's the metadata that is automatically generated by the camera whenever a picture is taken, and which is subdivided either as file properties or EXIF, short for Exchangeable Image File Format.

File properties include information such as file name, creation date, resolution, color mode, and so on. I use much of this information when checking large collections of images and when sorting them into high- and low-resolution groups, RGB and CMYK sets, or simply alphabetical lists.

EXIF is standardized among the main camera manufacturers to embed universal technical information, or metadata tags, and includes information such as aperture and shutter speed, ISO rating, white balance, and so on. Some manufacturers have even begun to include GPS (global positioning system) functionality into their high-end models to record the exact location of each shot, but

this practice has yet to become widespread. Not all cameras record exactly the same categories of information—it varies between manufacturers—but what does get recorded can be read uniformly by cataloging software (see pages 066–079). As I mentioned above, much of the EXIF information is probably less useful to designers, who are simply looking for the right image. However, don't dismiss EXIF information, as there are aspects of quality control when selecting from a wide choice of imagery that could be influenced by EXIF data. For example, images shot with a lower ISO rating will have fewer distracting "noise" artifacts when printed.

Other types of metadata must be entered manually, so you need to decide as part of your image-management workflow just how much information you need. This is covered in greater detail later in the chapter (see pages 066–079), where we discuss the best methods for building a catalog of relevant images and embedding metadata. It's possible for a photographer to enter some of this information when first downloading new images from the camera to a computer, but this depends on which method the photographer is using and what type of software is available. For example, when cataloging software such as Expression Media (formerly iView MediaPro) or Extensis

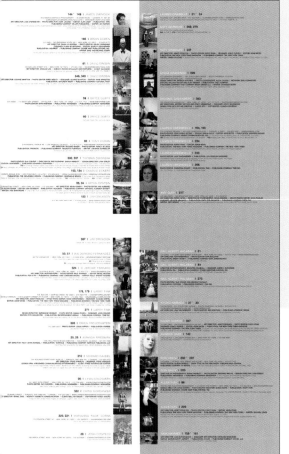

American Photography 17, a book showcasing the winners of the American Photography competition. Metadata can be used to match images to the contents list as part of your workflow, and can provide important information when captions or credits are added.
Design: 344 Design

Portfolio is running, it can be set to ask automatically if the photographer wishes to enter certain elements of metadata. Using this method will embed the same data in every image downloaded during the session, so data entered in this way has to be universal. For example, a photographer could add a standard copyright note to all his images during every download. In the same way, information such as a job code or project title could also be embedded in the metadata at this point, enabling you to link images to specific projects without having to input the data manually later in the process.

Image by image

Prior to the widespread use of digital cameras, image selection and organizing took place around a lightbox. Now the same procedure can be carried out on-screen using any of a wide choice of software, entering image-specific metadata as you go. For example, during the course of an initial image-selection process images can be star-rated and tagged with information using either browser or catalog software. A big advantage provided by digital technology is that a catalog can easily be distributed electronically to many different members of a creative team via the Internet, intranet, or e-mail.

Again, when deciding what information to embed, try to keep it simple—you won't want to waste a lot of time plowing through unnecessary data, and there are many information fields that aren't particularly relevant to the organization of a typical design project. Ultimately it's for you to decide what you need for the image catalog; but to get you started, the following spread details the data fields that I begin with for most projects. The headings refer closely to Adobe Bridge, as it normally provides the start point for my image workflow, but most browser and cataloging software will feature similar fields. ➔

⊖ What is metadata?

File Properties

Much of the information displayed under File Properties is drawn directly from the data embedded in the image itself. A glance over the file properties will tell you all you need to know about format, resolution, and color. The assigned label and rating fields are also displayed under this category.

Label

Labels can be customized in the preferences of most browser and catalog software. This is very useful as a sorting device in listed views, allowing you to easily group images with the same assigned labels together with one click.

Rating

A star rating indicates to other team members which images are first or second choice, and so on. This can be particularly useful when despatching material to out-of-house designers who will make independent choices of images to include in a project.

IPTC Core
Creator/Source

It's possible to forget during a project where images have originally come from. Purchased images may already have this information embedded, but any images obtained from other contributors should be tagged with this information in order to avoid confusion when organizing acknowledgments or payment. The creator corresponds to the original photographer or illustrator, the provider to the source of the material—which may or may not be the photographer.

Description

I use this field for a brief indication of the image's intended use. For example, one photographer may have provided material for three different sections of a brochure. The Description field can be used to indicate which images are intended for each section. The Description field is also useful when creating catalog sets later in the process.

Location

I actually use this field to indicate an image's destination in the first instance, which of course becomes its location once the image has been used. This is particularly useful when planning projects such as books or brochures, and provides the means to sort images into the sequence in which they'll appear in the final project.

Title

Enter the project title here rather than the image's actual name, which can be seen in the File Properties panel.

Job Identifier

Use this field to record a predetermined code corresponding to each project, to ensure it's possible to track stray images if they are mislaid on your workstation or server.

Instructions

Record anything that happens to be relevant here, such as special cropping or general usage instructions.

Rights Usage Terms

Some images may have been provided without full permission for use, pending a decision from you with regard to their inclusion on your project. Use the *Rights Usage Terms* to record whether or not written permission to use the material has been received.

Keywords

Generally I don't go so far as to add keywords, this being more for photographers with huge collections of images that they may wish to make commercially available. It is, however, a feature that may well be useful, depending on your circumstances.

◪ This screenshot indicates the maximum range of metadata that I might work with. For a simple project I may only use the IPTC Core field. Decide for yourself how much information you need for your own workflow.
Photography: Terry Dear

Digital image catalogs

Having covered naming procedure and explored filing and metadata, it's time to discuss image catalogs. A digital image catalog is *the* best way of selecting, keeping track of, and managing all the images for a given project. But before making a catalog, ask yourself, "Is it really necessary?"

As a rule of thumb, if there are more than 30–40 images and they need to be referred to regularly by a number of people, then it's probably worth creating a catalog; if, however, there are relatively few images which only need to be viewed by you and perhaps one other person, it's probably only necessary to keep the images stored and logically filed on your workstation or a server, and use an image browser to view, select, and manage the images.

Browsers vs. cataloging software

Image browsers, such as Adobe Bridge, differ from cataloging software in that browsers don't store data in the form of a saved file. Instead, they access information about images whenever they are pointed at them. Because browsers can't store data in the form of a saved file, they can't create permanently accessible catalogs. Cataloging software, on the other hand, creates a permanent store of digital information in a file that can be duplicated, edited, and distributed independently of the original image files that it's being used to manage.

Browsers

Prior to the release of Adobe Photoshop v. 9, or Photoshop CS2 as it's otherwise referred to, the File Browser provided the means to view and launch images via a browser-style interface within Photoshop. This has now been replaced with Bridge, a much more powerful stand-alone browser, which also provides access to Adobe Stock Photos, where high-quality stock images can be sourced and purchased.

I use Bridge as an image-workflow alternative to the Finder because it allows you to search for and view images more efficiently. All the information you may need about an image is easily accessible via the metadata panels, and new data can be quickly and easily embedded in image files for later use. You can see a large preview of any selected image, and you can add star ratings to images as part of a selection process. Remember, though, that Bridge can't create permanent catalogs for remote reference. If you move the images to another drive or archive them to CD or DVD, they're out of Bridge's reach. This could be seen as a disadvantage, but not every project involves hundreds of images to keep track of and sometimes, as long as the browser can "see" the images, software such as Bridge is all you need. ⊟

⊟ Adobe Bridge is likely to be the most familiar image browser to most designers, due to its inclusion in the Creative Suite. The latest version, CS3, has added some useful features, including a loupe magnifier for checking details within the preview pane.
Images: Vault 49

Vault49

List | Thumbnail | Media

Dedicate-p2-3_1479.tif 7.0 x 4.6 cm | 1 MB | TIFF

Media Info

Media Type	Image
File Type	TIFF
Encoding	TIFF (LZW)
File Size	1 MB
Disk Name	seddon
Orientation	Default
Dimensions	7.0 x 4.6 cm
Resolution	300 pixels/inch
Depth	24 bits
Compression	1:1
Color Space	RGB
Color Profile	Adobe RGB (1998)
Pages	1
Created	28/07/06 17:09:35
Modified	29/12/06 17:24:51
Archived	29/01/07 17:09:09
Annotated	29/01/07 17:12:36
Thumbnail Size	34668 bytes
Annotation Size	162 bytes
Metadata Size	123016 bytes
Recording Size	0 bytes
Source Software	Adobe Photoshop CS3 Macintosh

Annotations

Title	Images: A creative digi...flow
Creator	Vault49
Source	Vault49
Copyright Notice	© Vault49
Job Identifier	V1479
Rights Usage Terms	Grant of rights received
URL	www.vault49.com
Location	Unassigned
Instructions	TBA
Status	TBA

Keywords

Double click to add keyword...

Description

Catalog 4.8 MB | Media 45.1 MB

Complex-ad_2_2_1479.tif

Complex-ad2_1479.tif

Fall-AD-2_3_1479.tif

McD-1-4_1479.tif

Camel-music-mailer-6_1479.tif

Dedicate-1_1479.tif

Dedicate-p2-3_1479.tif

Dedicate-p4-5_1479.tif

Dedicate-p6_1479.tif

Digit-Mag-Green_1479.tif

INDEPENDENT_Corruption_1479.tif

INDEPENDENT_Decay_1479.tif

31 items in list | 1 selected [7]

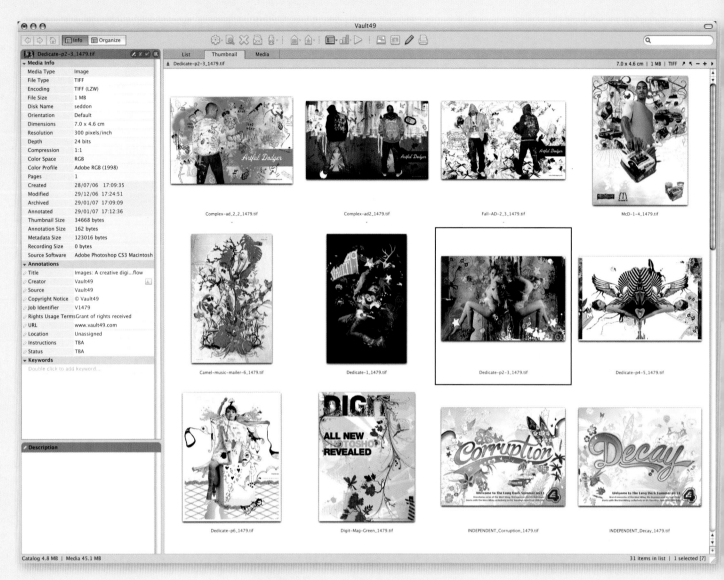

Cataloging software

If you need to organize and distribute large numbers of files permanently, however, a browser is less useful. Cataloging software can save information out to a database file, which can subsequently be used more flexibly as part of an image workflow. Let's take a look at the advantages offered by cataloging software.

The creation of a digital catalog will, of course, require an investment of time, but once completed, accessing the images for viewing and searching will be much faster than it would be with a browser, as all the data is stored in that single database file. A browser may have to look repeatedly through hundreds of folders before it can provide a result. Another significant advantage of cataloging software is the ability to create *catalog sets*. These sets can be organized using an endless range of criteria to suit your particular image workflow. No duplication of image files is required for this, as the contents of sets all link back to the original files, allowing individual images to appear in as many different sets as required. You can also easily save the contents of catalog sets out for distribution or backup, preventing the need to visit numerous folders spread across your various drives or network.

A lesser-known advantage that can be a real saver is that, if a cataloged image is accidentally deleted from your workstation or moved to another disk or server, the image's record remains in the catalog and is tagged as "missing." A browser couldn't flag this problem, as it would simply no longer "see" the image, but cataloging software will raise the alarm and allow you to replace the deleted image from your backup (as long as you have been practicing good backup procedures, that is!).

Finally, and significantly, you can share image catalogs with colleagues and clients for selection and approval regardless of their geographical location, and without having to send the original image files. As long as they have a computer, they will be able to view your catalogs on-screen quickly and easily. Cataloging software companies also provide "reader" applications (in principle like Adobe's Acrobat Reader) that can be distributed freely with prepared catalogs, which means your clients don't have to purchase their own copies of the software in order to view the catalogs in their original format.

◧ A catalog of images, such as the example here made using Expression Media, can be freely distributed to creative team members and clients. A feature for creating web galleries, plus tools for the automation of many image-related tasks, makes software of this type integral to any serious digital image workflow. *Images: Vault 49*

Creating image catalogs

So you've decided that an image catalog will help in the running of your project; what next? What software should you use, and how should you to use it?

I choose to use Expression Media (formerly iView MediaPro) for my catalogs as I think its feature set and ease of use are well suited to my own working methods, and to most creative design project structures. For this reason, the examples included here show the Expression Media package. However, there are other well-established products, including Extensis Portfolio, which are worth considering. Please remember, therefore, that much of what I discuss here can be achieved regardless of software choice. I highly recommend researching, downloading, and testing trial versions of all the available creative asset management products before you decide which one will suit you best.

Catalog-building strategies

Before you create your first catalog, decide on the number of catalogs you need. Should it be one big catalog of all the images you've got, or should it be kept to one catalog per project? If I were a photographer I would probably go for the single catalog option, thus maximizing the value and accessibility of my material in its entirety. But as a designer I think the one-catalog-per-project option is the better choice. You could maintain a separate catalog, with relevant subsets, of images that you own outright and

may want to use in more than one project, but the chances are that the majority of the images you're using at any given time will relate to specific projects. Here are some strategies you may want to consider when building your catalogs.

By project

Another advantage to creating a separate catalog for each project is that it enables you to monitor a project's progress closely by tracking the images you've received at key points in your schedule.

By subject

Creating subject-based categories is usually performed either by image content or by category, or both. For example, you could create catalogs for all your travel-based material, or you could narrow this to all travel images that contain shots of beaches. Theme-based subjects such as "favorites" or "dominant color" can also be useful. The important thing is to ensure that there are no major overlaps, so always endeavor to create unique categories for all your images to help you keep track of your material.

By task

Your workflow is likely to contain a series of key image-manipulation procedures, so separating these into individual catalogs that represent these stages can help directly with the management of your image processing. An example would be unedited RAW images, moving to selected images, moving to color-balanced and sharpened TIFFs for repro, moving to archived returns. This method is better suited to a photographer's typical workflow, but if you shoot any of your own material it's a useful approach.

By chronology

Catalogs of images acquired within predetermined time frames (monthly, annually, etc.) are useful as part of the process of building a large, searchable archive of all your material. These can be created by importing material from existing project catalogs. It's worth noting that Expression Media, for example, can search all the catalogs stored in one particular folder. If you store all your chronological catalogs in one location you achieve a complete, searchable archive with no extra effort. ⇒

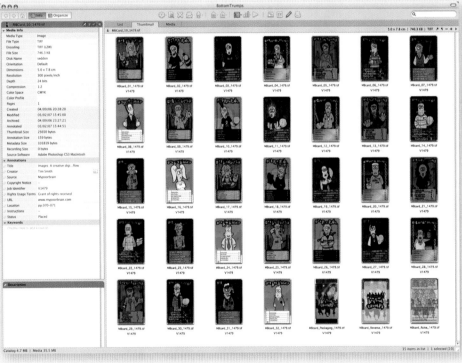

⬆ Cataloging a project incrementally during its schedule will help you to monitor progress, particularly if you're commissioning or producing material over a restricted time period, as was the case with this student design competition brief.
Design: My Poor Brain

⊙ Creating image catalogs

Making the catalog

My procedure for building a catalog from scratch in a folder (or folders) of new, untreated images is broken down into these stages:

1 Review all images in Bridge to ensure there's no additional material to source for the project.

2 Perform renaming procedures and convert images to your required file format (see pages 094–095).

3 Embed a standardized set of organizational metadata using Bridge.

4 Import selected images into a new or existing catalog.

5 Enhance catalog as required with additional metadata.

6 Produce contact sheets in the most suitable format for the project.

7 Distribute the catalog to the rest of the creative team.

Keeping it simple is the main objective. If the process gets too complicated it'll seem more trouble than it's worth, and you won't want to do it at all.

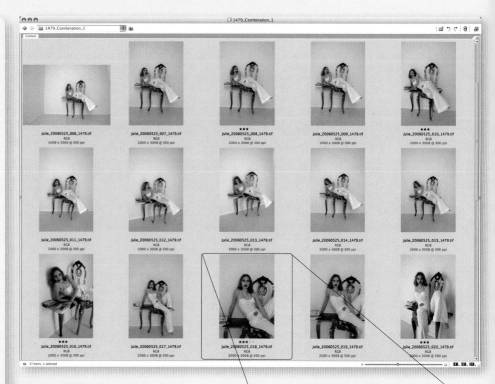

The browser stage

This is where the browser comes into its own, acting as a powerful replacement for your standard desktop or Finder. I've trained myself through force of habit to go straight to the browser I use, Bridge, whenever I receive a batch of new images for a project, so I can make a visual assessment of all the material right from the outset. If the material isn't suitable for your needs, or isn't what you were expecting in any other way, you can stop right there and get back to your supplier to discuss things without performing any unnecessary procedures on the files.

Julie_20060525_018_1479.tif
RGB
2000 x 3008 @ 300 ppi

⬆ I set Bridge to its Light Table view option for the first run-through of new material, as the assessment is purely visual at this stage. Also, if any images stand out I rate them with three stars as an indication of their likelihood for selection. This rating can be upgraded later in the selection process.

Photography: Jason Keith

If I'm happy with the material, the next stage is to do any necessary file conversions. These are likely to change elements of the file names, even if it's only the file type, so later changes would require extra updating of your catalog. These conversions are not strictly part of the catalog build, so I'll cover this area in more detail later in this chapter (see pages 100–129).

Bridge has a well-featured batch-renaming facility, which is sufficient for most requirements. When the renaming requirements are complex, I tend to use it in combination with a piece of software, called A Better Finder Rename, that offers a more specialist set of renaming options (see page 059). The amount of work needed here will

depend a lot on how the files have been named when supplied to you. If they already have their own unique names, it can make things easier, but you may run into problems if file names are duplicated, say between folders that are delivered in separate batches. This is where there's no substitute for a bit of logical thought and methodical sorting through of the material. Refer to What's in a name (see pages 058–059) for tips on how to structure your file naming. ⏎

(see pages 100–129). (see page 059). (see pages 058–059)

TIP

You can either use a Photoshop Action to convert a large number of images easily from one format to another, or the Image Processor script supplied with Photoshop. There are nearly always several ways to carry out a task, so be sure to investigate them all as part of you own workflow strategy.

⬆ The Batch Rename functionality offered by Bridge is very flexible and will cater for most designers' needs. If you need more features, look at a third-party software package such as A Better Finder Rename.

Photography: Jason Keith

⊖ Creating image catalogs

Once you're happy with your file naming, you can begin to add metadata to your image files. Information added to images within Bridge is embedded as XMP (Extensible Metadata Platform) metadata, meaning that it stays attached to the files when they move between workstations and across platforms. The choice of metadata fields provided by Bridge can seem daunting at first. It corresponds to the full standard as laid down by the IPTC (International Press Telecommunications Council). These standards are periodically updated to include any new metadata requirements that arise from the latest technological advances. To create a more streamlined image workflow for the average graphic-design project, fields that are not required can be hidden in the preferences of both browser and catalog software, making it easier to focus on the specific information you want to use.

◀ ▲ Without metadata the cataloging process wouldn't be possible. It can be added to images via the XMP panels, accessed via *File > File Info*. Alternatively, a metadata template can be created from data already embedded in a selected image, as shown left.

Photography: Jason Keith

Metadata templates

Bridge allows you to store frequently used metadata field entries as metadata templates. To create a metadata template in Bridge, open an image and go to *File > File Info...* to access the XMP information panels. Enter any metadata you want to include, and save a template using the drop-down menu in the top right corner. Alternatively, a template can be created from metadata that's already embedded in an image via the pop-out menu at the top right of the metadata pane (see screen shots above) and used to add metadata to additional images. Metadata templates created in Bridge are fully compatible with MediaPro as well as all other packages that support XMP, and can be appended or replaced at any time.

You may decide after experimenting with this method that you would rather skip the Bridge stage and go straight to the catalog software of your choice. I've adopted the Bridge to MediaPro method because I often receive material for each separate project that I'm working on in lots of different ways, at different times, and in considerably different degrees of organization. Adding a standardized set of metadata entries before you get stuck into the cataloging procedure

means you don't have to remember so much about the origins of each and every image, and can concentrate more on building a really well-organized catalog, and on entering additional metadata that is more relevant to the project as a whole. ⊡

⬆ Any images added to a workflow can easily be updated with the correct metadata using a template created using metadata from another image in the set.
Photography: Jason Keith

⊕ Creating image catalogs

The catalog stage

Now that your images are named, formatted, and carrying some basic metadata, full cataloging can begin. At this point, the reasons why adding some metadata in Bridge is advantageous should become apparent. If you've followed my method, you'll be able to import a large collection of images, filed within grouped or nested folders, into a new catalog with a single process. Tracking the origins of these files would be difficult without the metadata you'vse embedded. You could, of course, import each folder from your desktop into a new catalog individually and add data for each in turn, but I don't find this a very efficient way of going about the process.

You can import material (not just images, incidentally, but also audio, video, DTP, text, and illustration) by dragging files into an open catalog window. This is good for small numbers of files that are being added to an existing catalog, but I generally prefer to import items using the appropriate menu. This allows you to add items directly from a connected camera, external drive or disc, URL, Spotlight Query, an existing catalog, or of course, from a specified folder. It also allows you to add metadata from an existing metadata template as part of the import, which is useful when cataloging any images that you've shot yourself.

Now you have your catalog, what do you do with it? The first consideration is to look at how you can further enhance the information to work best within your image workflow. I often find it useful to adapt my standard configuration of the view options during any one given project depending on the information I need to view, but for consistency I always start with a default setting for each option, which is shown in these screen grabs of Expression Media.

You'll notice that there are now a few more metadata fields visible at the left-hand side of each screen than during the Bridge stage. This is the template I first apply to all Expression Media catalogs I create. Copyright notice, URL, and status are useful items of ongoing information that tend to become available once the creative process begins, so it makes sense to add this information after the catalog has been built. I'm certain that you'll form your own preference for the default settings that suit you best, and of course it's not essential that this extra information is added to your catalogs. ⊕

⬆ Importing images by dragging them to the Expression Media window is practical if you are adding just a few at a time, but for large numbers of images in nested folders it's easier to use the *File > Import Items > From Files/Folders* ... menu.
Photography: Jason Keith

TIP

If you're importing images directly from a camera, think about applying metadata to them immediately, using a template that you've already created in either Bridge or Expression Media.

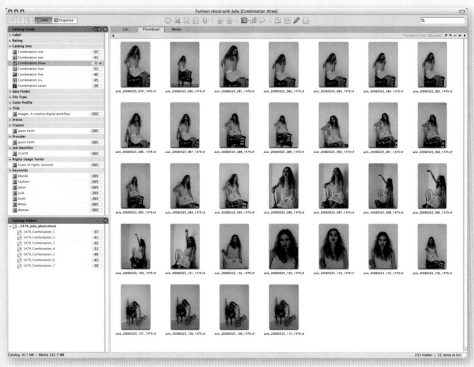

The Organize options provide a number of useful ways to filter the images you want to view. Creating catalog sets (top) of distinct groups of images is useful for filing or editing your images, and groups can be viewed in isolation by clicking on the button next to each set's name (above). Note that images can also be sorted by their original folders from which they were first imported, using the same method.

Photography: Jason Keith

⊖ Creating image catalogs

Contact sheets & distribution

The advantages provided by creative asset management technology are many and varied with regard to on-screen functionality, but for ease of reference it's still difficult to beat a printed contact sheet. You can scribble notes on it, give it to someone else so they can scribble more notes, and what's more it doesn't require a power supply. Most cataloging software is capable of producing contact sheets, and you can configure the number of images per sheet and the metadata information that appears next to each image.

I always include a printed contact sheet as part of my brief when I hand over material to freelance page make-up designers, to help them locate each image easily. A listed picture log in text form is also useful when sending out artwork to repro houses or printers, and can aid communication if any problems arise.

The *Text Data File* function in Expression Media is ideal for this. The required metadata fields can be customized, and the resulting file can be imported into a third-party database or spreadsheet package. The only

disadvantage of printed material is distribution—you have to use the mail or a courier, slow by today's standards.

There are some excellent electronic alternatives to a printed contact sheet. The simplest option is to export contact sheets in JPEG form, which you can then e-mail as attachments. Expression Media has a built-in function that fully automates the process. Alternatively, you can export an image catalog as an HTML (Hypertext Markup Language) gallery. Expression Media has fully customizable options for embedding annotations and metadata, making life much simpler. Once uploaded to a web server, your catalog works just like a website and can be accessed by anyone with an Internet connection. All you have to do is e-mail the URL to your creative team members or clients. I particularly like this method, as the catalog can be regularly updated at any point in the project without sending out new files, and there are no restrictions on the number of people who can be given access to the catalog.

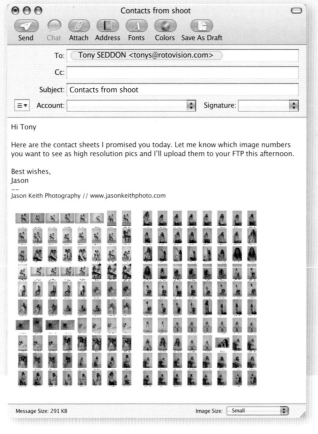

◪ E-mailing contact sheets generated from your cataloging software is a very quick and easy way of distributing images for selection. Remember that Photoshop can also generate contact sheets in this way.
Photography: Jason Keith

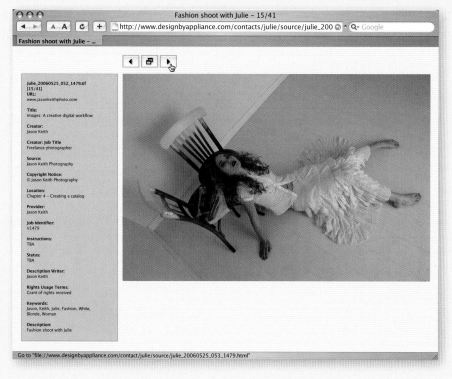

A cataloging conclusion

What you've just read is, of course, only one way of putting catalogs together. It suits the kind of publishing projects that I'm generally involved in, and it's not so complicated that it can't be adapted easily when required. My advice is to look at the thinking behind this method, and then experiment in order to form your own procedure that best suits your needs. I'd be surprised if my preferred settings were just right for everybody, but that's the beauty of using good creative asset management software as part of your image workflow. It gives you the freedom to customize and adapt constantly to the changing needs of each project, while maintaining a consistent method and approach. As I said in the Introduction, if you think of the cataloging process as part of the creative work rather than as part of the administration it won't seem like such an onerous task. Your efficiency will increase, and you'll have more time for creative work.

⬆ Creating an HTML gallery which can be posted on your web server is the easiest way of all to get your images seen by the largest number of people. The template shown above is built into Expression Media, and allows users to click on any thumbnail to see a larger preview alongside all the embedded metadata. This is a great way to work collaboratively, and can even be used as a way of distributing low-resolution positionals to freelance designers, as they can save previews to their own desktop for use in a layout.

Photography: Jason Keith

The image process workflow

So far we've discussed planning and sourcing images, and how to construct a catalog that tells you where each image came from and where it's going to be used. This next section looks at the practical aspects of understanding how the color information and resolution of a digital image affects how it reproduces when printed or viewed on-screen.

Scanners & scanning

Despite the wide use of digital cameras, and despite the fact that most image libraries now supply digital files rather than transparencies or prints, scanners are still very much a part of most image workflows.

Once the domain of repro houses and print shops due to the prohibitively high cost of the hardware, high-quality scanning with affordable devices in-house is now common practice; even inexpensive, home desktop scanners can produce surprisingly good results. There are three main types of scanner in regular use today—flatbed, film, and drum. A full description of each type can be found in the glossary. Flatbed scanners are the most commonly used, due to their low cost and versatility, and are probably the type with which you're most familiar.

Practical considerations

The maximum resolution, or sampling rate, at which a flatbed scanner can capture an image is specified by a pair of figures, such as 4800 x 9600ppi. The first figure here, derived from the number of fixed sensors present in the scanning head, gives the sampling rate across the horizontal width of the scanner's bed or glass plate. The second figure indicates the highest sampling rate at which the scanning head can move along the vertical length of the bed, stopping to sample each line. The lower of the two figures gives

Scanning small originals

If you're scanning a small original such as a 35mm transparency, to get the best results check the size at which you wish to reproduce the image and scale it up at the scanning stage. If your scanning software doesn't feature a scale setting, multiply the percentage enlargement you require by the output resolution needed—usually 300ppi for print—and increase the resolution of your original scan accordingly. Remember not to exceed the true optical resolution of the scanner.

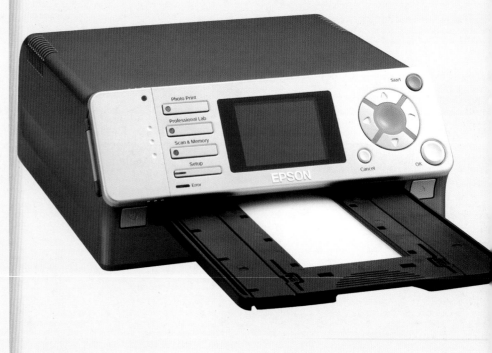

↑ If scanning transparencies is a frequent requirement, a specialist film scanner like the model shown is an excellent option. Batch scanning with film holders makes the task much easier, and scan quality is very high thanks to accurate color profiling and a dedicated lamp system.

the true optical resolution of the scanner, so it's best to avoid trying to scan anything at a higher sampling rate. Higher resolutions require software interpolation, which generates extra pixels to fill the gaps that the scanner can't actually record. Detail isn't improved when using interpolation, and the file size is made unnecessarily larger.

To scan or not to scan?

Don't run away with the idea that you'll be doing all of your own scanning from now on. If you have a large number of images to scan and the quality must be high, it's better to negotiate a price and send them to your repro house or print shop. It may be cheaper to scan out-of-house when you take into account how much *chargeable* time it would take to do the work yourself, and the quality of the end results will be someone else's responsibility. You can always reject scans and request that they be redone if you're not happy with the quality.

⬆ With an optical resolution of 4,800 x 9,600dpi, scanners like the model shown can produce scans of a very high quality which are suitable for most print applications. Large-format transparencies can be scanned using a film adaptor, and Digital ICE™ technology can be used to restore damaged originals.

Color models

Without color models, or color spaces as they are also known, it would be impossible to move digital images through an image workflow with any degree of consistency. Color models provide us with a mathematically based system (don't worry, you don't have to do the math) that translates real-world color into a form that can be reproduced accurately on screen and in print.

Color models are either device-independent or device-dependent. Device-independent models are essentially more precise when describing any one color as they don't need to reference a specified output device. Such models, LAB being a prime example, mimic the way the human eye perceives color. Device-dependent models differ in that they are designed to provide the numerical values that allow images to be reproduced consistently by monitors, printers, and printing systems. RGB and CMYK are the most commonly used examples of device-dependent models, appearing as a part of pretty much every image workflow. The colors reproduced on screen or in print using device-dependent models are governed by the characteristics of whatever hardware you

utilize. They're limited to the range of colors, known as the gamut (see Color gamut panel on page 086), that your devices are capable of producing. This does of course mean that the colors you see using this type of model are not necessarily "true" colors, but they will be consistent throughout your workflow so long as you don't change your hardware halfway through. Besides, if the true color can't physically be reproduced as part of your final output there's no point in being able to see it in the first place.

In addition to color models, color profiles are crucial to achieving consistency across a managed image workflow. I'll discuss profiles and color management in more detail later (see pages 088–089).

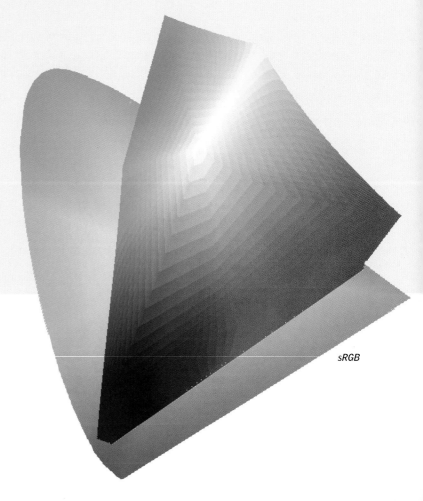

sRGB

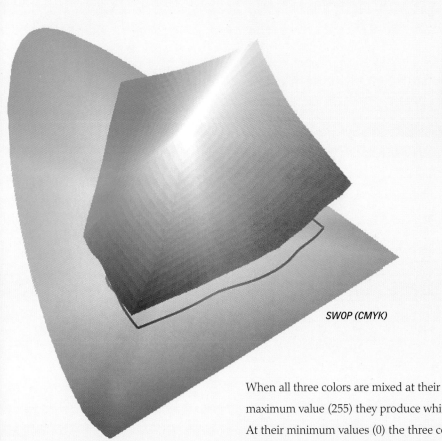

SWOP (CMYK)

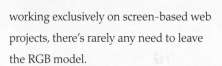

Common color spaces defined

There are three color spaces that are commonly used in the great majority of print and on-screen projects.

RGB (device-dependent)

RGB is the model used by all computer displays, and describes color as emitted light. Each pixel in each of the three separate red, green, and blue (hence RGB) channels of an RGB digital image is valued on a scale ranging from 0 to 255. The additive primary colors (see Additive & subtracting mixing panel on page 087) of red, green, and blue are mixed with differing values to create different colors.

When all three colors are mixed at their maximum value (255) they produce white. At their minimum values (0) the three colors create black. On a 24-bit display, 16,777,216 (256 x 256 x 256) discrete combinations of hue, saturation, and luminosity can theoretically be created. In practice, fewer distinct colors are actually produced, but still many more than the human eye is able to differentiate.

You'll probably use RGB more than any other color model when working directly with images, particularly as a large number of Photoshop filters and functions will only work in RGB. I tend to leave images in RGB for as long as possible during print projects, and certainly keep original RGB versions of all material as well as any RAW files (see pages 102–107) if I have them. If you are working exclusively on screen-based web projects, there's rarely any need to leave the RGB model.

CMYK (device-dependent)

CMYK describes colors using percentages of the subtractive primary colors cyan, magenta, and yellow. Mixing 100% of all three colors should theoretically make black, but in practice, due to ink and paper limitation, the result is actually a muddy brown. Therefore, black (which is also referred to as the key, so providing the K in CMYK) is added to the mix to increase the density of color in images and tints. Black is of course also required to print clearly readable black text type. The color gamut of CMYK is smaller than that of RGB, so any intensive color correction work should be completed before the CMYK conversion is carried out. ⊟

⊠⬆ The 3D diagram to the left represents the commonly used sRGB color space. The diagram above shows the SWOP (Specification for web Offset Publications) CMYK color space used extensively by the US printing industry.

⬆ This diagram directly compares the two spaces, with the sRGB space overlaid as a wireframe, indicating how much smaller the CMYK space actually is. These diagrams were created using Chromix ColorThink.

→ Color models

Color gamut

A color gamut represents the full range of colors that any one specific color model is capable of defining, or the full range of colors that a device can capture or display. All computer monitors display color within the RGB gamut, while color in commercial printing, such as the color images in this book, are represented by the CMYK gamut. Because the RGB gamut is larger than the CMYK gamut, not all the colors represented on screen can be achieved in print.

LAB (device-independent)

Originally named L*a*b*, but now commonly referred to as LAB, this model is made up of three channels that combine together to describe color. The L represents luminosity, the A represents color on an axis from red to green, and the B represents a corresponding blue-to-yellow axis. LAB provides the interchange space that allows programs to display and reproduce color accurately between devices. For example, Photoshop converts RGB images to CMYK by first moving them to LAB mode. This is because, as well as having a larger gamut than other models, LAB is capable of separating an image's luminance from its color. This provides greater control over tonal and color correction, not just when moving between models but also when manually color-correcting an image in Photoshop.

This sounds perfect, so why not just use LAB all the time? Well, there are a couple of significant drawbacks. First, input and output devices aren't matched well to LAB; in other words, cameras and scanners don't use LAB to represent color and printers don't use it to reproduce color. Second, if you're working in Photoshop and are using Layers combined with LAB, you'll have to flatten your image when converting back to RGB.

To make full use of LAB you need to feel very confident and familiar with all aspects of color correction, and you need to be sure that any color work you've carried out will be retained when converted back to RGB or CMYK. So, do your homework and run some tests to determine how well you know the model before committing yourself to any serious work. Once you're completely familiar with its characteristics, you'll find that working with LAB can often produce the most satisfactory results.

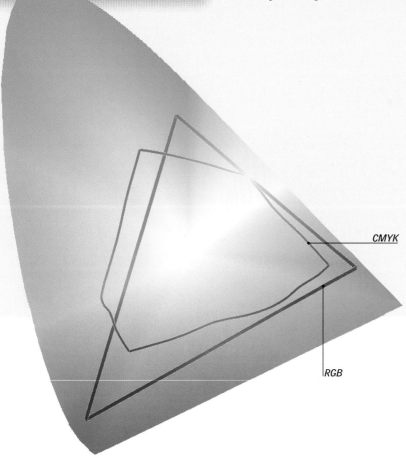

CMYK

RGB

◨ This is a simplified 2D version of the 3D comparison diagram on the previous page. The RGB and CMYK color spaces are shown within the much larger visible color spectrum. You'll notice that there are areas at the corners of the RGB space that aren't covered by CMYK. These are the colors lost during a conversion from RGB to CMYK.

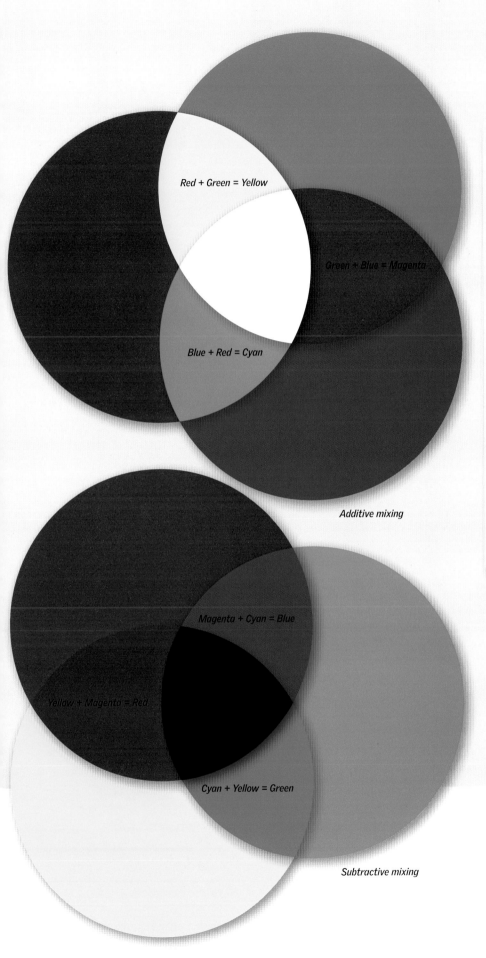

Red + Green = Yellow

Green + Blue = Magenta

Blue + Red = Cyan

Additive mixing

Magenta + Cyan = Blue

Yellow + Magenta = Red

Cyan + Yellow = Green

Subtractive mixing

Additive & subtractive mixing

Put simply, when it comes to color theory additive involves light and subtractive involves pigments. Additive mixing is what happens on a computer's display, where red, green, and blue light combine to form colors. Subtractive mixing happens when inks, or pigments, printed onto a surface absorb particular wavelengths of light depending on the pigments used. The resultant reflected light creates different colors. Considering how different these two processes are, it's no wonder that there are often considerable color differences between on-screen images and those in print.

↑ ↖ The additive mix (top) involves red, green, and blue light mixing to form white, with yellow, magenta, and cyan light forming as secondary colors. The subtractive mix (left) involves cyan, magenta, and yellow pigments absorbing light to reflect different colors. Cyan only absorbs red, magenta only absorbs green, and yellow only aborbs blue.

Color profiles

Every designer has at some stage experienced problems with inconsistent color because of the differences between devices (such as scanners and printers) in a workflow.

However, help is at hand in the form of color profiling. A color profile is a file containing data that describes how any one device will behave when it deals with color information. There are three types of profile—input, display, and output—and they work by representing colors as device-independent numerical values.

The images you work with are most likely either RGB or CMYK, both of which are device-dependent color models. They work with additive (RGB) and subtractive (CMYK) primary colors (see page 087), where the color values describe directly how much of each primary color makes up the color of each pixel on a computer screen or dot in a printed color image. However, if you use different printers with different types of ink or paper stock, these variations mean your images won't reproduce consistently. Profiles help to achieve consistent colors because they utilize a device-independent color model such as LAB (see page 086). All input profiles contain a table of comparative values that translates the colors in an image to the device-independent color model, known as the Profile Connection Space (PCS). The values can then be translated back to device-dependent color values via a display or output profile, maintaining color consistency. To retain the ability to translate values accurately throughout an image workflow, images should be saved, or tagged, with the required profiles. Color-management software (CMS) built into applications can interpret the tagged profiles at any point in the workflow.

Input and output devices generally ship with dedicated "generic" profiles produced by the manufacturer. They're pretty accurate but they don't take into account the small manufacturing differences between each device, or changes due to wear and tear. If you require absolute color accuracy, your devices should be profiled using specialist equipment and techniques.

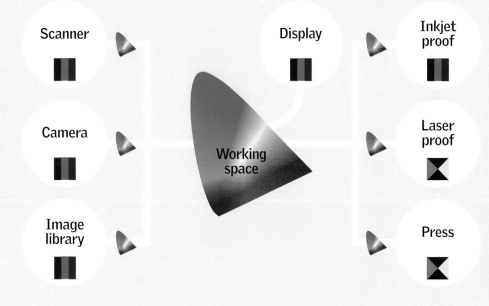

Scanner

Camera

Image library

Working space

Display

Inkjet proof

Laser proof

Press

➤ Color profiles used effectively in a managed workflow allow you to control color between all your input and output devices. A wide-gamut working space, for example, Adobe RGB (1998), must sit at the center of your workflow to act as a link between all devices.

The International Color Consortium

The technology behind color profiles is based on standards set out by the ICC (International Color Consortium), which was established in 1993 by Adobe, Agfa, Apple, Kodak, and Sun Microsystems. If you'd like to know more about the ICC, a wealth of information is available on their website at www.color.org.

Creating your own profiles

Creating custom profiles is a complex and time-consuming process, particularly when you're calibrating printers, so think carefully before investing in expensive kit. It may actually be more cost-effective to pay a specialist consultant to do it for you.

Displays are particularly susceptible to change over time. At the very least, creating a profile for your monitor by eye using system software or a third-party software solution is a worthwhile exercise and will help to maintain accuracy over a longer period of time. The on-screen instructions that take you through the process are easy to follow. Two factors to bear in mind are the color temperature and the screen gamma. I find a 6500K (or D65) color temperature is good for most Mac working environments; any higher is too bright and doesn't accurately reflect images once they're printed. Apple's default gamma setting is 1.8, while Windows recommends 2.2. This creates cross-platform problems, where Mac users' images will appear darker and more contrasty when viewed on a PC, and Windows users' images will appear washed out on a Mac display. When designing for the web, lighten darker images slightly if you're a Mac user, and darken bright images slightly if you use Windows. It's a compromise, but will generally produce the best all-round results.

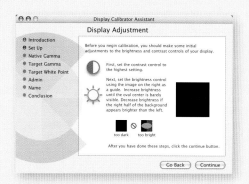

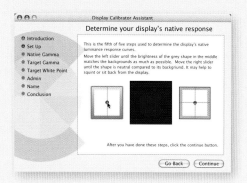

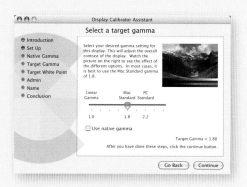

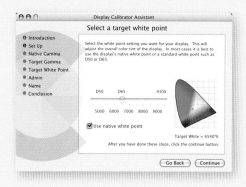

⬆ If you're using a Mac it's possible to create your own profile for your display, using the system software. On-screen instructions make it a simple process, and it's well worth doing every so often in order to maintain accurate color on your display. A control panel with a similar function is available to users of PCs running Windows.

⬆ Specialist solutions, such as the Blue Eye calibration device from LaCie, provide automatic hardware calibration and ICC profiling.

Photoshop color settings

It's important to make a decision about color settings before preparing images for use in layouts. The following is a guide to each area of Photoshop's Color Settings dialog box (accessed via *Edit > Color Settings*).

1. Settings

Adobe provides a range of standard printing presets for Europe, the United States, and Japan. These, along with any customized settings saved to your hard drive, can be accessed from this drop-down menu.

2. RGB working space

When first introduced to color management, I was wrong in assuming that this was the place to specify your display profile; in fact it represents the RGB working space. Adobe RGB (1998) is a good choice as the default setting, as it has a wide-gamut profile that won't limit the amount of color information available to you.

3. CMYK working space

If your printers can provide you with a custom profile for their press, use it for the CMYK working space setting. Otherwise, use a preset to achieve the best generic match. Europe ISO Coated FOGRA27 or U.S. Web Coated (SWOP) v2 are good choices depending on your location.

4. Gray working space

If you're working on images for use as part of a website, choose a suitable gamma for Mac or Windows. For print-based projects, check with your printers to ascertain the amount of expected dot gain (see Glossary) for their press. Grayscale images are not otherwise color managed.

5. Spot working space

Spot colors are produced by mixing specific proportions of process inks, and so cannot be color managed. Once again, check with your printers for the correct amount of dot gain to specify.

6. Color management policies

If images are supplied complete with embedded profiles, Photoshop needs to be told whether they are to be retained, amended to your default working space, or ignored. I choose to preserve them for all image types, and decide once an image is open if a change of profile is the best policy to implement. It's a more controlled approach, and alternative profiles can be assigned at any time if necessary.

7. Mismatched & missing profiles

Photoshop can be prompted to ask what to do if any of the policies set in color management can't be met. If you produce layouts for both print and the web, you may want to keep different RGB profiles assigned to images intended for either print or online use, so maintain complete control by keeping

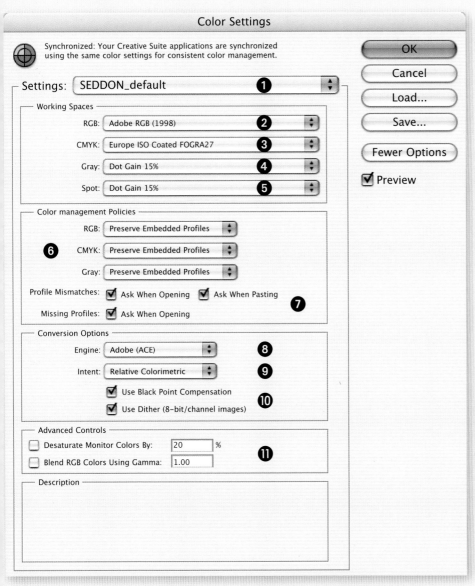

9. Rendering intent

See pages 092–093.

10. Black Point Compensation and Dither

Checking Black Point Compensation means the black in an image will be mapped to the black point set by your chosen output profile, so the full range of tones from black to white (or paper color) will be achieved. Checking Use Dither aids color blends and prevents banding when converting 8-bit images from one color space to another. I keep both these options switched on.

11. Advanced controls

Colors outside the gamut your monitor is capable of displaying may appear more distinct if you choose to desaturate your display, but inaccuracies in the overall look will probably result. Switching on Blend RGB Colors Using Gamma displays blends as "light" rather than "ink." I tend to leave both advanced options unchecked.

all three of these boxes checked. Incidentally, the Missing Profiles checkbox refers itself to untagged images with no profile embedded. If you always use the same profiles for every single image you handle, you can uncheck these boxes.

8. Color management engine

The Adobe Color Engine (ACE) is the default setting and works well in most circumstances. Custom color engines from third-party sources may also be utilized within alternative specialist workflows.

Rendering intents & out-of-gamut colors

As we've discussed, a gamut is the complete range of colors that any one specific color space is capable of producing. Because the RGB color space is bigger than CMYK, there'll be colors within images that will be outside the gamut of some output devices and so can't be reproduced.

The original image

This situation is dealt with by Rendering Intents. The Intent options are found in the Color Settings dialog box (*Edit > Color Settings*) under Conversion Options. It's important to understand what the choice of method produces during the transition from the RGB to the CMYK color spaces.

Perceptual

This method attempts to preserve the visual relationship between colors by compressing them into the gamut of the output profile. This does tend to alter most of the colors in an image, including those that the output device could have reproduced accurately. It can also cause images to lose color saturation, but does produce the best results for images that contain a large number of out of gamut colors.

Saturation

This method doesn't alter colors that the output profile can produce accurately. Colors out of gamut are changed, but the priority is to maintain the saturation of the color rather than the hue. Therefore, some colors may change quite significantly, which isn't ideal for photographic images. The method is more useful for preparing charts and diagrams where the actual colors aren't so important.

Absolute Colorimetric

This method also maintains colors within the output profiles gamut, but changes out-of-gamut colors to the closest hue possible, sometimes producing a slight loss of saturation as a result. This sounds ideal, but there are potential problems to be considered. Absolute Colorimetric attempts to reproduce white areas from the input to the output in exactly the same way, so will nearly always add at least some color to white areas, producing a color cast. It's a useful method for proofing with a device that has a larger gamut than the final output device you wish to mimic, as ink added to the white areas may help simulate the color of the printing stock.

Relative Colorimetric

This is the method to use for most situations, and is the default setting in Photoshop. It's similar to Absolute Colorimetric in most respects, differing only in that it adjusts the white point of the input profile to that of the output profile. Therefore, it produces results that are close to the original image and is the best choice for prepress work.

Perceptual

Saturation

Absolute Colorimetric

Relative Colorimetric

 These four portraits have all been converted to CMYK from the same original, but a different rendering intent has been used each time. The differences between each image are indeed subtle, but there are slight shifts towards the expected results in each. For example, Absolute Colorimetric has produced a color cast.

Photography: Jason Keith

Common file formats

Image files destined for use as part of a layout must be saved in a specific type of format, identified by the three-letter suffix at the end of the file name, such as .jpg, .tif, .pdf, and so on. Each file format has its own characteristics, with some being more appropriate for use in print and others for use on-screen.

Your image workflow may be entirely print orientated, or it may comprise a combination of drawing, page layout, and screen. The repurposing of material originally created for print for use on a website (see pages 170–171) or as part of a multimedia product is now common, so you must be clear about which format is appropriate for which media. The glossary at the end of this book contains full definitions for commonly used file formats, but here is an overview.

EPS (encapsulated PostScript) and TIFF (tagged image file format) files are popular choices for use in print projects. Data of various types can be embedded in the files and read by the page make-up software of your choice. For example, InDesign and QuarkXPress can both read alpha channels embedded in a TIFF, and consequently, gradations around objects created in Photoshop can be imported directly into layouts with ease.

The JPEG format (Joint Photographic Experts Group) is frequently used for both print and screen, but care must be taken when deciding how much compression should be used. If small file size is the most important issue, use as much compression as possible, but if the job is destined for print, exercise caution, as the quality of the end result will be seriously impaired by too much compression.

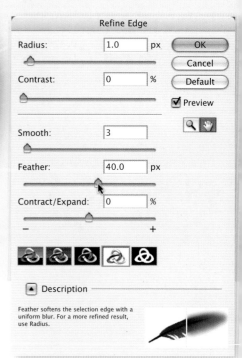

⬆ The feathered alpha channel, shown as a selection in the screen shot to the left, has been used to create the vignette edge of the above image directly in InDesign. The new Refine Edge function in Photoshop CS3 was used to adjust the feathering by eye.

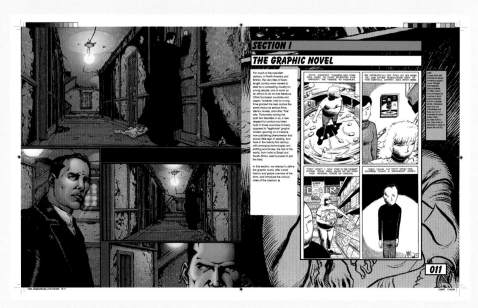

The PDF (portable document format) has, to an extent, edged out the EPS format, as PDFs can contain just as much information but provide other advantages besides, including support for transparency and a comparatively small file size. PDF is the file format of the moment, accessible to all through the free Acrobat Reader, and widely supported. File formats specific to web usage are discussed on pages 172–175.

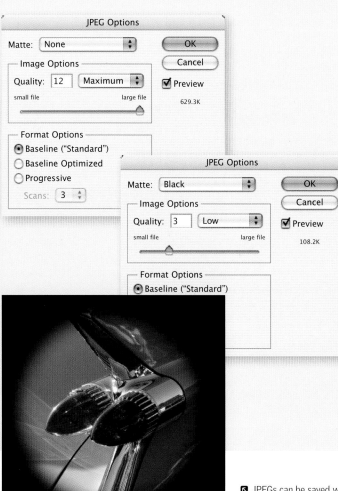

It's important to consider the compatibility factor when making decisions about which formats to use in your image workflow. Resaving files to another format halfway through a schedule is never a rewarding process. For print, you should liaise with the repro house and printer to determine what will work best for them, particularly if your job contains any vector graphics (such as those created by Illustrator, for example), as these can be the most problematic. If there is a chance that the material might be reused for an on-screen project, you've got a choice of JPEG, GIF, or PNG, all of which help to keep file sizes low through compression.

◪ JPEGs can be saved with varying degress of quality. The lower the quality, the greater the compression and consequent reduction in file size. The Matte menu can be used to add a selection of backgrounds to transparent areas of an image if required.

↥ PDF is the ideal format to use when supplying complete press-ready artwork to printers.
Design: Studio Output

Bit depth, resolution & image size

The kinds of images that you might typically use in a project can vary from simple black and white to full color. It's the amount of information contained within each pixel which determines both the type of, and the quality of, each of those images.

Bit depth

Bit depth is the number of bits (binary digits) assigned to each pixel that makes up a digital image. It contributes to the quality of an image, but in terms of color rather than resolution, which we'll come to in a moment. Put in simple terms, the higher the bit depth the more tones can be achieved, so gradations and subtleties in color will increase as the bit depth increases.

1-bit

Black-and-white images, in which each pixel is either on (black) or off (white), are 1-bit images. Line art that doesn't require any form of tonal gradation can be 1-bit, but it must be of a sufficiently high resolution to prevent jagged edges appearing. For print, 1-bit images should be at least 300ppi (pixels per inch) or more to prevent this occurring (see Resolution & image size on page 098). For screen use, a resolution of 72ppi is sufficient.

RotoVision

8-bit (24-bit)

Black-and-white photographic images that include smooth tonal gradations are 8-bit images; they use 8 bits of information for each pixel. An 8-bit grayscale image is capable of producing a total of 256 different tones ranging from white to black. Full-color images are also sometimes referred to as 8-bit, but technically they're 24-bit because the three RGB channels (see page 085) have 8 bits each, giving a total of 24 bits of information per pixel. With the 256 possible tones combining for each channel of each pixel, just under 16.8 million colors can be theoretically achieved—256 x 256 x 256 = 16.77 million. Quite enough for anyone, but an even higher bit depth is achievable.

⬆⬈ The 1-bit image above has been saved with a 150lpi screen set at 45° to retain detail in the midtones. This can also be achieved using dithered black and white dots (see Glossary). The RotoVision logo is also a 1-bit file, produced as line artwork in Adobe Illustrator.

16-bit (48-bit)

Photoshop has for some time been capable of editing 16-bit (or strictly 48-bit) images. Although many effects filters will not work, image adjustments such as Levels and Curves will. It's worth undertaking color manipulation work on 16-bit images if they're available—even though some of this extra information may not be reflected in the printed result—because gradations and tones will look more refined. However, because the file sizes of 16-bit images can be large, work with them until all manipulation is completed, then convert them to 8-bit before placing them in a layout. ⏏

◄ These two images are both designated as 8-bit. However, the color image is technically 24-bit, as it contains 8 bits for each of the three RGB channels.

Photography: Jason Keith

↑ This image is designated as 16-bit, or 48-bit, depending on your terminology. There is more color information in it than in its 8-bit equivalent (shown left), but the limitations of print make it difficult to show this on paper. However, the slightly higher red "peaks" in the overlaid histograms show that the 16-bit image (in red) contains more information than the 8-bit (in black).

Photography: Jason Keith

⊖ Bit depth, resolution & image size

Resolution & image size

The relationship between resolution and image size is fairly straightforward, but it's important to understand how one affects the other. A digital image can be produced with either a scanner or a camera at a *specific* resolution set by the device, but when used and resized in a print or web layout this original resolution doesn't remain constant. The *output* resolution is determined by how many pixels per inch (ppi) appear in the image when it is printed or displayed, and this in turn determines quality. A recorded

pixel doesn't magically reproduce and multiply when the image is enlarged in a layout; the pixels themselves are enlarged and therefore become more visible, and consequently the quality of the reproduction is reduced.

Let's look at a couple of specific examples. Start with an image 6in wide which has been scanned at 300ppi, the standard resolution for good-quality printing. This image will measure 1800 pixels across: 6 x 300 = 1800 pixels. When imported into an InDesign or QuarkXPress

layout at 100% of its actual size, it will reproduce at 300ppi. However, if you enlarge it to double its size in the layout, the resolution will halve to 150ppi. The same applies when low-resolution images are reduced, but in reverse. I have a camera that records images at 72ppi, but the original image size is large at 3456 x 2304 pixels, or 48 x 32in. If this image is reduced to approximately 11.5in wide it will reproduce at 300ppi, giving a high-resolution image and a print size that is large enough for many publishing uses.

100% / 300ppi

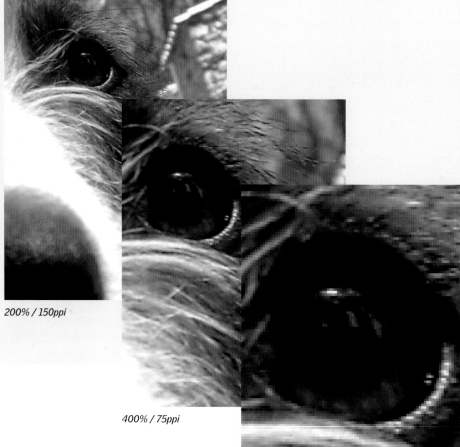

200% / 150ppi

400% / 75ppi

800% / 38ppi

⬆ ➚ This rather fetching portrait of Mungo the dog is reproduced here at 300ppi and at 100% of its original size. The image is sharp and no individual pixels are obviously visible. When incrementally enlarged "in-layout," the actual resolution decreases and the pixels become increasingly evident.

Photography: Tony Seddon

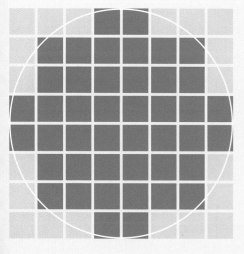 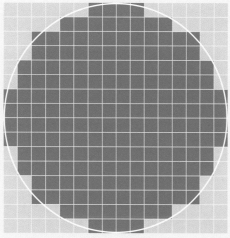

Screening

A printed image, or halftone, is made up of a matrix of equally spaced dots that vary in size to produce color and tone. "Screening" is the term used to describe the process of creating a halftone from a continuous-tone image. When selecting which halftone screen resolution to use, the type of printing and paper stock to be used must be taken into account. For example, high-quality stock such as that used for this book, will utilize a screen of between 150 and 170lpi (lines per inch), whereas a newspaper printed on lower-quality paper will use a screen of between 70 and 80lpi. The coarser screen helps to prevent the individual dots from merging together due to ink spread through the more highly absorbent paper.

The relationship between image resolution and halftone screen resolution works like this. Image resolution should be roughly twice the halftone screen resolution, hence the standard 300ppi with a 150lpi screen. It's possible to get away with images of a lower resolution, but it does depend on the image's content. Sharp images with lots of fine detail are less forgiving than softer images with large areas of color and tone, and pixelation (where jagged edges become visible) can occur if too much license is taken with original image resolution.

↑ Halftone dots can be represented graphically. On the left is a halftone dot of 8 x 8 pixels giving 64 grays. On the right, a higher-resolution dot of 16 x 16 pixels will produce the Postscript maximum of 256 grays.

Image resizing in Photoshop

When an image is resized in Photoshop, the software either discards or creates pixels depending on whether you are resizing the image up or down. Downsizing an image will not reduce quality, as Photoshop doesn't have to create new information that's not already in the image. Upsizing an image is of course possible, but a reduction in quality is inevitable, as Photoshop has to create new pixels through resampling. However, if you have to enlarge an image, do it in Photoshop before you place it on the page. This is discussed in more detail on pages 120–121.

Too much resolution

Using images at a resolution that's much higher than is necessary, i.e. 300ppi for halftones and 600ppi for line work, will not necessarily improve the quality of the final output. Banding (see Glossary) can occur in areas of continuous tone if an image's resolution doesn't correspond favorably to the halftone screen used; furthermore, overly large file sizes will slow down all prepress processing and overstretch your storage and backup facilities.

Image adjustment

The following pages discuss techniques that will enable you to work with Camera RAW and DNG image files, and methods you can utilize when adjusting and improving your images. As this book isn't solely about Photoshop, I've concentrated on only the principal adjustment tools that might fit into a typical image workflow. Best practice for resizing and sharpening images is also covered here, along with a brief look at vectors. For those readers who haven't upgraded, or are planning the transition from Adobe CS2 to CS3, both versions are discussed comparatively in this section of the book where relevant.

Working with Camera RAW

The majority of photographic images you are likely to work with will be supplied as TIFFs or JPEGs, but occasionally you may receive RAW images straight from the photographer. Darkroom techniques, chemicals, and paper can be combined to produce a range of alternative image results from a film negative, and a RAW file is the digital equivalent of a film negative.

It contains all the raw data that is recorded by the sensor in a digital camera, as well as all of the camera's settings at the time the photo was taken. Unlike a JPEG, a RAW file is not compressed in-camera, so file sizes are larger. Furthermore, as files are not subjected to any in-camera processing, complete control over the final result is in your hands. Temperature adjustments (for white balance), tint, exposure, and a whole range of additional parameters can be set at the point at which you first open a RAW image. To open a RAW file you'll need the Camera RAW plug-in for Photoshop, or a stand-alone application from your camera's manufacturer. RAW files can also be opened from within Bridge.

There are drawbacks to using RAW files. For one thing, they aren't standardized as the format of each is governed by the make and model of the camera on which it was shot. Your image-editing software may drop support for older cameras over time, meaning you'll no longer be able to open your original RAW files.

They also work in conjunction with sidecar files, which are small text files automatically saved to the same folder as the original RAW image. The sidecar file records and remembers all the settings applied to the RAW file each time it's

opened. If you lose the sidecar file or move the original RAW files to another workstation, you're back to square one. It's true that RAW files provide a wealth

◪ The new version of Camera RAW which ships with Photoshop CS3 has undergone a few changes. The Workflow Options are now edited via a separate window, and a raft of new adjustment sliders have been added. A useful visual guide to indicate what the effect will be when the sliders are moved to the left or right has also been added.
Photography: Jason Keith

of advantages over other image formats. However, there is an alternative to RAW which is a little more flexible and offers the same benefits—Adobe's DNG format. ⊟

⬆ For those of you yet to upgrade to CS3, here is the CS2 version of Camera RAW for comparison. The controls allow an extensive range of adjustments to be made to the RAW file prior to opening or saving, but are not as flexible as the newer version.

Photography: Jason Keith

TIP

Set your Camera RAW preferences to apply sharpening to Preview images only. It's best to use dedicated sharpening filters (see pages 122–125) when you've completed all post-production work, as at this stage you don't know what additional adjustments the image will undergo. The preferences are accessed from the Toolbar in CS3, or by clicking on the small black arrow at the top of the Settings palette in CS2.

→ Working with Camera RAW

Camera RAW & other formats

The new version of Camera RAW which ships with Photoshop CS3 is capable of opening both TIFF and JPEG files, opening up a whole new way to approach the image-editing workflow. Just remember that not all the benefits of a RAW original, which is "untreated" data, can be drawn on when opening an alternative format. For example, enlargements from a JPEG original will not be of the same quality as those generated from a RAW original.

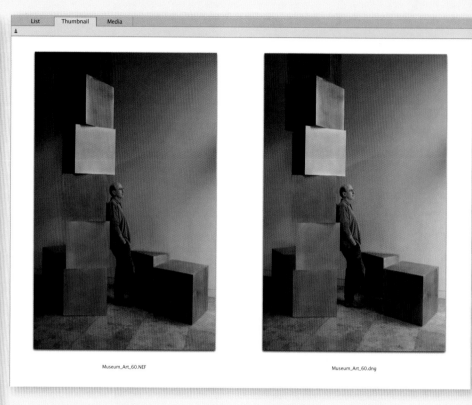

Museum_Art_60.NEF   Museum_Art_60.dng

The DNG alternative

I really like the DNG (digital negative) file format. Adobe devised and introduced it as part of Photoshop CS2 in order to standardize the format in which original RAW images can be stored. DNG files are generated via the Save option in the Camera RAW plug-in, and contain all the data from the RAW original. They're self-contained in that they don't require sidecar files—a much neater solution—and the file sizes are smaller due to lossless compression options offered as part of the Save procedure. However, the biggest advantage involves the cataloging stage. Cataloging software such as iView doesn't read sidecar files, so image adjustments can't be seen in RAW file previews. DNG files are different in that they are previewed accurately, providing a huge advantage within the digital workflow. If you're using Photoshop and RAW files frequently, consider the option of saving the RAW images that you intend to use to the DNG format and ditching the RAW originals.

⬆ Both the images above, displayed in an iView MediaPro catalogue, have undergone the same adjustment process. However, the RAW file on the left doesn't reflect any of those changes. The DNG file, on the other hand, is previewed accurately with all adjustments visible on screen.

Photography: Jason Keith

It's an extra stage to build in, but I think the workflow is improved as a result. I should mention that DNG files can't be opened with third-party software from all main camera manufacturers, but some do support the format, so check compatibility first if you don't have Photoshop CS2 or CS3 along with Camera RAW.

Using the Camera RAW plug-in

Beginning at the top left of the Camera RAW dialog, you'll find a set of basic tools for navigating, cropping, rotating, and so on. There's also a white-balance eyedropper tool, which is handy for quick adjustments to images where areas that should be neutral are visually obvious; and the Color Sampler tool is useful if you need to compare color values in different areas of an image. In addition to the tools, you'll notice a checkbox named Preview. This allows adjustments to be previewed as they're made, with warnings

displayed in the form of a color overlay for any areas where adjustments are clipping detail. I find this option very useful, and keep it checked all the time when working with Camera RAW. This replaces the three separate checkboxes—Preview, Shadows, and Highlights—found in the older version of Camera RAW which shipped with CS2.

The Workflow Options of the Camera RAW plug-in palette, now in a separate window called up by clicking on the link-style text at the base of the palette, control the main attributes for the image to be generated from the RAW original. Let's take a look at each one individually.

Space

I always set this to the RGB color space that I have as my Photoshop default, Adobe RGB (1998); this ensures the image is ready for further adjustment in Photoshop once the file has been converted.

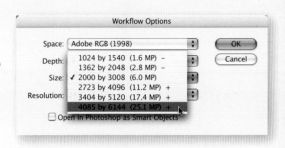

Depth

Select either 8 or 16 bits per channel here. (Bit depth was discussed on pages 096–097.)

Size

The number of options available here will depend on the camera used to take the shot. Note the "+" and "–" signs after each option; these indicate the increase or decrease in image size using interpolation. Because a camera's sensor records single colors with each of its individual photodiodes, Camera RAW will produce pixels with greater color accuracy when interpolation is utilized to resize a captured image. Therefore, if you know you want to enlarge an image, now is the best time to do that.

Resolution

This setting won't affect the physical dimensions of your image, so it's best to set it to whatever is required as the final output resolution, usually 300ppi for press or 72ppi for screen. ⊟

↑ The Color Sampler tool can place markers at various points in the image, sampling the color and providing an accurate RGB breakdown. This is particularly useful when carrying out very fine color adjustments.

Photography: Jason Keith

↑ The number of Size options will vary from camera to camera. The Nikon D70 used to take our example RAW image gives us five additional options: two reductions and three enlargements.

⊕ Working with Camera RAW

Adjustments

The tabbed palettes at the right of the Camera RAW screen provide a host of options for controlling image adjustments. The Adjust (CS2) or Basic (CS3) tab is the one I use the most when opening RAW files.

White Balance

This determines the image's color balance, based on the color temperature of the light source under which the image was shot. Auto and As Shot will give the same result if the camera's white-balance setting can be read by Camera RAW. Alternatively, if the camera's white-balance setting has resulted in a noticeable color cast, you can select another option from the presets. This feature is unchanged in CS3.

Temperature & Tint

In this context "temperature," like "white balance," refers to color temperature. The slider is used to compensate for unwanted color casts caused by color temperature; moving the slider to the left compensates for a low (red) temperature and therefore makes the image bluer, while moving the slider to the right compensates for high (blue) temperatures and makes the image yellower. The Tint slider should be used to fine-tune the image, and basically adjusts the color

balance from green on the left to magenta on the right. Again, this option works the same with CS3, but the sliders are now colored to remind you what effect an adjustment will have on an image.

Exposure

The numerical value here corresponds to f-stops, where a + value represents opening up the aperture of a camera's lens to increase exposure, and a – value represents closing down the aperture to reduce exposure—in other words, it adjusts the brightness of an image. You can ensure that detail isn't lost through clipping when brightening an image by using the Preview (CS3) or Highlights (CS2) checkbox to indicate blown-out areas. The Exposure slider itself hasn't changed in function with CS3, but the Recovery slider below is a major addition. It allows you to increase the overall exposure, which may create blown highlights, and then recover only those highlights without adjusting the exposure back down. This is very useful for brightening images without losing lots of detail in the process.

Shadows, Fill Light & Blacks

The Shadows slider in CS2 has now become Fill Light with CS3. Its function is pretty similar: moving this slider to the right

intensifies all shadow areas, but to my mind it seems to do it that much better in the new version. Again, be sure not to lose detail through clipping when using the Preview

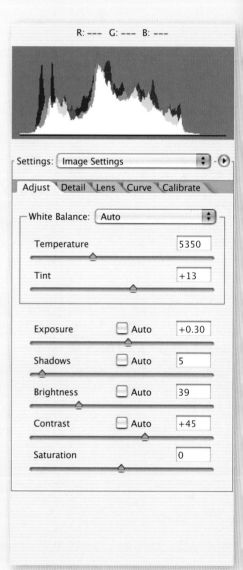

⬆ The Camera RAW adjustment panel from Photoshop CS2. Note the Auto checkboxes which can be switched on or off for each individual slider.

(CS3) or Shadows (CS2) checkbox. The new Blacks slider saturates only the blacks in an image rather than overall color, and is useful if you want your image to look more punchy.

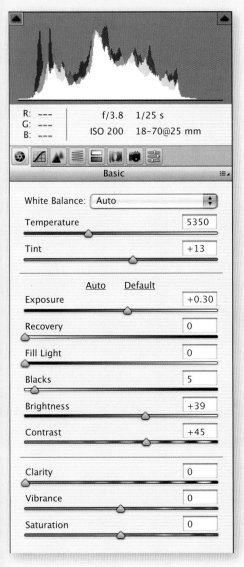

Brightness

Not to be confused with Exposure, this setting differs in that it doesn't affect black and white points (see Levels, pages 109–111). You can use it to fine-tune the image visually after adjusting Exposure, but I tend to leave that until later in the workflow, where better tools are available.

Contrast

Again, I tend to leave this setting alone, as it may otherwise wipe out color information that you'll need later in the adjustment process.

Clarity, Vibrance & Saturation

CS3's new Clarity slider increases local contrast, providing a great method for quickly adding depth to an image. The new Vibrance slider effectively replaces the Saturation slider, and is much smarter, as it only increases the saturation of unsaturated colors, leaving the already saturated colors alone. The Saturation slider is still there, but I prefer to leave this set to zero. It can wipe out detail overall, so any adjustment is best left until later in the workflow when you can utilize an adjustment layer (see page 111).

The rest of the tabs provide advanced settings better suited to discussion in a book dedicated solely to Photoshop; it's rare that

I change any of these camera defaults at the RAW stage, at least in the context of my average digital image workflow. However, the new Parametric option under the Tone Curve tab is well worth a look, as it allows you to make tonal adjustments using the sliders beneath, providing a very intuitive way of adjusting overall tones straight from the RAW original.

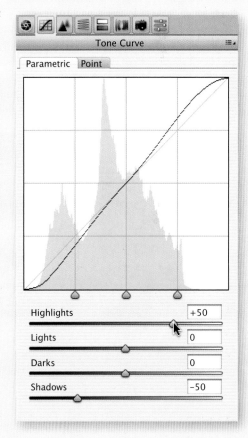

Basic tonal & color adjustments

Here's the scenario. You've got a selection of images to choose from and you find the ideal shot among them, but unfortunately it's not perfectly exposed. Maybe the shot is too dark, or perhaps it's lacking in contrast, but you really want to use it. Let's look at how to fix the problem, starting with the basic adjustments.

Priorities

There's no set order for making specific types of adjustment—it depends entirely on the image. I find that tonal adjustments are needed more often than any other type, and therefore I tend to make these adjustments first. A tonal adjustment affects the brightness and contrast of an image. Often you'll find that an image's color is also affected as a result of a tonal adjustment—saturation will increase or decrease when darkening or lightening an image—but essentially this is about brightness and contrast.

Brightness/Contrast

I don't use the Brightness/Contrast adjustment for anything beyond the most simple of corrections, on such things as quick visuals and the like. I view Brightness/Contrast as an all-or-nothing adjustment, as it doesn't discriminate between shadows and highlights that well, which isn't ideal for the majority of images. Admittedly, Adobe have made improvements in CS3 and the sliders now work similarly to their equivalent in Camera RAW, but a Levels adjustment will provide better, more controlled results.

⬆ This night shot of a café is mainly shadow with a few bright highlights. The Levels palette histogram reflects this with a distinct bias towards the left. Note the sharp peak at the far right, indicating the clipping that has occurred in the bright highlights on the metal chairs.

The loss of detail in these bright areas isn't a particular problem in this case, but spikes at either end of a histogram are something to watch out for.

Photography: Tony Seddon

TIP

If an image needs some attention before it can be used, decide what the worst issue is and deal with that first. It may be all that's needed to fix the image completely.

Levels

For me, using Levels is a visual exercise—despite the fact that input and output levels are displayed numerically within the dialog box—and I always opt to work with the Preview box checked. Once you've mastered Levels, I doubt you'll think about using Brightness/Contrast again, even for simple adjustments. The Level command's major advantage is that it allows you to adjust the contrast within the shadow and highlight areas of an image independently, and to adjust the brightness independently of those shadow and highlight settings.

The histogram plays a key role in Levels adjustment, and it's important to understand its function. The shape of the histogram indicates how tonal values are distributed throughout an image, running from shadows on the right (the black point) to highlights on the left (the white point). If the histogram is biased toward the right, for example, your image will be predominantly dark. A left bias will conversely represent a bright image.

The histogram also indicates how much clipping has occurred in an image. "Clipping" is the term used to describe how much information, and therefore detail, has been lost in the shadows and highlights of an image, and shows up as flat areas at either end of a histogram. A distinct spike at the highlight end of a histogram can indicate clipping in bright reflections from metal or glass. The ideal image shouldn't exhibit any clipping, particularly in the highlight areas, where detail is most often lost. To fix the problem, create a Levels Adjustment Layer (see panel on page 111) and begin by adjusting the positions of the black and white point sliders, moving them inward so they sit below the beginning and end of the existing histogram, that is, the point at which the graph reaches zero. This action will redistribute the range of tonal values between the darkest and brightest points. If the image now has too much contrast, move the sliders back out a little and reappraise the result, repeating until you're happy with the image. ⇥

⬆ Although the tones in the original shot (inset) are reasonably well distributed, clipping has occurred at either end of the histogram. Dragging the black and white point sliders inwards to align with the ends of the histogram produces a more pleasing result overall.

Photography: Tony Seddon

Basic tonal & color adjustments

The middle slider below the histogram adjusts the midtones within the image, and is often thought of as a brightness control. Moving the slider to the left sets the mid-gray point closer to black, and produces a brighter image, while moving it to the right has the opposite effect and makes the image darker. Remember, moving the mid-gray point won't alter the position of either the black or white points, so overall contrast remains good.

If you wish, you can also use the Levels adjustment for color adjustments by selecting individual channels from the drop-down menu. However, I normally turn to the Color Balance command for color editing.

Color Balance

The Color Balance dialog is the easiest method provided by Photoshop for basic color adjustments, such as the removal of color casts. The three sliders represent each of the three color channels—red, blue, and green—and are helpfully labeled to indicate the relationships between the opposite additive and subtractive colors. It's a common misconception that, for example, the cyan/red slider only affects cyan/red pixels and so on. This isn't true. A Color Balance adjustment affects all pixels in an image, unless you're working with a selection.

⬆ The midtone slider is a very effective brightness control. Move it to left to brighten (top), or to the right to darken (bottom) an image. The main advantage with this method is that the black and white points remain fixed, so detail is preserved.

Photography: Tony Seddon

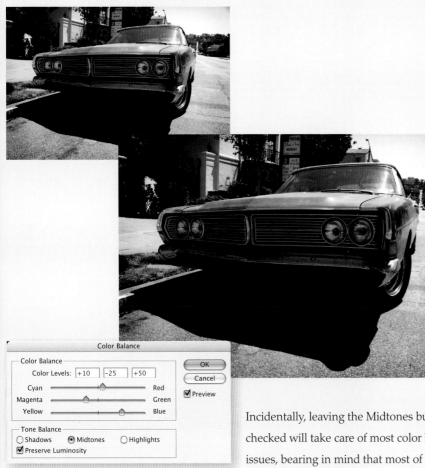

TIP

Whenever possible, use an Adjustment Layer for all correction procedures. Created via *Layer > New Adjustment Layer* or by clicking on the pop-up menu in the Layers palette, an adjustment layer allows corrections to be made without permanently affecting the original image. This means you can backtrack or readjust images without committing to changes until you're sure you have the desired result. Furthermore, you decide how the various adjustment layers interact with one another, and images can be saved and used with their adjustment layers intact or merged for final output. If adjustment layers aren't supported for the adjustment you want to make, create a duplicate layer instead and make your adjustment to the duplicate—that way you'll always retain the original.

When making a Color Balance adjustment, first adjust the slider that will affect the image most significantly. For example, if an image has a strong yellow cast, start by moving the yellow/blue slider to the right, assess visually what effect that's having on the image, and proceed from there. It's likely that you'll overdo it initially in order to ascertain what's needed, so be prepared to pull sliders back to a position that creates a more pleasing overall adjustment, and remember to take advantage of the Adjustment Layer feature.

Incidentally, leaving the Midtones button checked will take care of most color balance issues, bearing in mind that most of the tonal range will be within this area. Finally, keep the Preserve Luminosity button checked, as this will make small compensatory adjustments that will preserve the luminosity of all the colors in the image.

⬆ Moving the yellow/blue slider to the right removed most of the strong yellow cast from the original image (top), but the overall color was helped further by adding a little red and taking out some green.

Image: iStockphoto.com

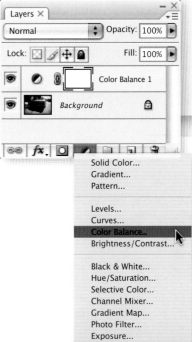

111

Advanced tonal & color adjustments

Assuming that the majority of images you handle are likely to be either commissioned or purchased, and therefore of a high original quality, basic tonal adjustments should be able to handle most of your requirements. However, if you're really serious about getting the best out of your images, the more advanced adjustment features offered in Photoshop provide many more possibilities.

Shadow/Highlight

Some Photoshop purists regard the Shadow/Highlight adjustment as a quick-fix tool, but personally I think it's indispensable for rescuing detail in problematic shadow and highlight areas. In the past I've managed to fix images using Shadow/Highlight that I'd given up on prior to its introduction as part of the CS2 release. In its unexpanded form, the Shadows: Amount slider is for brightening dark areas, and the Highlights: Amount slider

is for darkening bright areas. Those two sliders on their own can quickly transform a problem image by bringing out detail, and if you don't go overboard with the amount of adjustment, a good level of contrast is maintained. It's best to apply these two settings first until you're reasonably happy with the image. However, keep Show More Options checked, as the real power of the Shadow/Highlight command lies in these additional options.

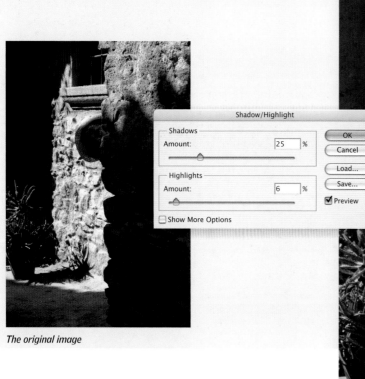

The original image

⬆️➡️ Using the two basic Shadow and Highlight sliders on their own produces a pretty good result. The shadow areas have been opened up considerably, but the brighter areas of the image, which actually looked fine before, are now rather washed out and the image is generally looking a little flat.

Photography: Terry Dear

In CS3, the additional sliders in the top two sections add options for adjusting tonal values. The Tonal Width sliders govern the range of values affected by the Amount adjustment, where a low percentage will only allow a narrow range of tonal values to be adjusted, and so on. This means you can fine-tune the areas of shadow or highlight affected. The Radius sliders govern the spread distance of the Amount adjustment, so they control how adjustments blend together.

The bottom Adjustments section provides additional fine-tuning functionality. The Color Correction slider effectively provides you with a way to adjust the levels of saturation in the darker areas of an image. Colors can look dull and faded in dark areas where there isn't enough light to bring the colors out, so a small increase in saturation can make a difference. The Midtone Contrast slider adjusts the contrast of those colors outside the shadow and highlight areas—and can produce some unusual effects if that's what you're after—but use the option sparingly to avoid unrealistic-looking images. Leave the Black Clip and White Clip at 0.01% in order to retain as much detail as possible during adjustments. ◿

◿ The additional options in CS3 have helped to improve both the shadow and highlight areas. The Tonal Width and Radius adjustments provide greater control over the range of values affected, and have allowed me to keep the bright areas close to the original while improving the shadows.
Photography: Terry Dear

113

⊙ Advanced tonal & color adjustments

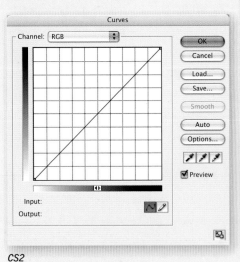

CS2

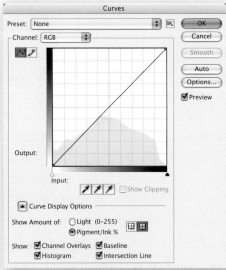

CS3

Tonal adjustments with Curves

The Curves command is undoubtedly the most powerful single adjustment tool in Photoshop. It's probably also the trickiest to master, but don't let that put you off using it. Curves works by adjusting all pixels at particular tonal values, where the values are selected and governed by the positions of anchor points on a curve (or line) above a grid—think back to the graphs you drew at school, where you compared values on the horizontal x-axis and the vertical y-axis.

Here the x-axis is the *input* value, and the y-axis the *output* value. You can also think of these as before and after values, which I prefer as it sounds less technical. Photoshop's default is to begin with a 45° line from

bottom left to top right, which effectively means no adjustment. If you take any one point on that line and move its position, the before and after values will alter according to the direction in which the point moves, and the image will alter accordingly.

The Curves palette has undergone a major overhaul in the transition from CS2 to CS3, but the principles behind its functionality are still the same. By default, the gradient for each axis runs from black to white for RGB images, but you can toggle this to run in the opposite direction by clicking on the gradient bar (in CS2) or by selecting your choice from the new Show Amount of option (in CS3). If an image is in grayscale, CMYK, or Lab mode, the gradient is automatically set to run

from white to black to represent added ink. I work in print and always think in ink terms, so I always set the gradient to run from white to black regardless of color mode: it's what I'm used to. All the points I make in this section assume a white-to-black gradient direction. The points at each end of the curve represent the white and black points, but if you've followed my suggestions you'll have set these already using Levels (the histogram makes it easier to do this with Levels), so leave the points at the corners of the grid.

The original image

◨ ⬆ The Curves palette has been given a facelift as part of the upgrade to CS3. The functionality is basically the same, but more information is immediately available by way of a displayed histogram.

Anchor points

In most cases you'll want to begin by seeing what effect a Curves adjustment will have on the midtones, so add an anchor point by clicking on the middle of the curve. The values indicating the anchor point's position in the Input and Output boxes will depend on the direction of the gradient, as Photoshop performs a neat trick here. If you're thinking like a photographer (with light) and have the gradient running black to white, the values conform to the standard 0–255 value range (see page 085). If, like me, you work with a white-to-black gradient, the values switch to a 0–100 value scale replicating percentages. I find this much easier to visualize because of my print background, but it's worth trying out both settings for yourself.

Back to that anchor point. An upward movement of the anchor point will darken the image, and a downward movement will brighten it. This is similar to the adjustment made with the midtone slider using the Levels command (see pages 109–111). A movement to the left will increase contrast, and a movement to the right will decrease it.

The sideways movements make the curve steeper or shallower, and you can relate this to the image. A steeper curve with its greater portion above the original 45° line means increased overall contrast, while a shallower curve will produce an overall decrease. Practice using Curves with a test image—it's the best way to learn what happens with each type of anchor-point adjustment. If using a color image proves to be confusing, try using a grayscale image first, as the specific adjustments you make will be easier to observe. ▣

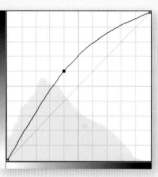

x = 40 (-10%)
y = 60 (+10%)

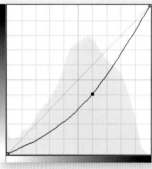

x = 60 (+10%)
y = 40 (-10%)

◤ ↑ The original image (left) has been split to show the effect of applying two different types of curve. The upper portion has been darkened and is more "contrasty," while the lower portion is brighter, with less contrast. In these examples, the anchor point has been moved by 10% in either direction.

Photography: Tony Seddon

115

Advanced tonal & color adjustments

The S-curve

The S-curve is a commonly used Curves adjustment that generally works well with most images. Its usefulness lies in the fact that it can increase contrast through the midtone range of an image without losing too much detail from shadow and highlight areas. To make an S-curve, add two anchor points 15–20% from either end of the default 45° line. Move the top point a little to the left, and the bottom point a little to the right, to form a shallow S-shaped curve. You should notice that your image now benefits from a boost in overall contrast but hasn't lost any significant detail. If you subsequently feel that the highlights could do with a bit more help, move the lower anchor point inward a little more, and so on, until you've achieved the desired result.

The original image

Color adjustments with Curves

Making color adjustments with Curves works in the same way as making tonal adjustments, the difference being that you make the adjustments to individual color channels, creating separate curves for each as required, instead of making one adjustment curve for the composite image. This ensures that you can deal with an imbalance of one color in the highlights and target a different color problem in the shadows, which would be very difficult to achieve using an alternative approach.

Assuming that you've taken my advice and kept your images as RGB thus far, you'll find on opening the Curves dialog box that

⬆ Applying an S-curve to our image has boosted the contrast in the midtones without losing too much detail in the shadow and highlight areas. The original image (inset) contains a little more detail overall, but lacks the drama of the adjusted version.

Photography: Tony Seddon

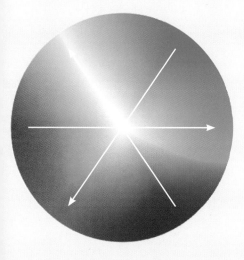

you can select each individual RGB channel from the drop-down menu at the top of the box. If your image happens to be CMYK, the channel choices will reflect this. To understand how an adjustment will affect an image, it's worth referring to the color wheel in order to remind yourself which colors are opposite one another. If you're working on the red channel, moving an anchor point upward will increase the level of cyan and moving it down will increase red. In the green channel, upward increases magenta, downward increases green. In the blue channel, upward increases yellow, downward increases blue. It's fairly straightforward in practice, and with careful placement of the anchor points it's possible to carry out color adjustments on a very specific range of tones within an image.

If you're not sure where the anchor points should be placed but can see from the image what needs fixing, click on the image's problem area and a circle will appear on the curve indicating the best position for the anchor point. If you click on the image while holding the Command key (Mac) or the Ctrl key (Windows), an anchor point will be placed on the curve in the appropriate position.

There are, of course, other adjustment methods provided as part of Photoshop's standard installation, but combining Shadow/Highlight and Curves will enable you to take care of most adjustments. Besides that, if an image is supplied requiring a more complex adjustment than anything described here, you should consider asking your supplier for a replacement.

⬆ This image's unpleasant green cast has been easily removed with a single adjustment of the green channel in Curves. Clicking on the rocky foreground where the cast was most pronounced revealed the best position for the anchor point, and a 7% increase from 25 to 33 has restored the natural color.

Photography: Tony Seddon

Smart filters

When adjusting images, the non-destructive route is always the best, if the option is available. Adjustment layers provide us with the means to make changes to color and exposure without committing irrevocably to the chosen settings, but until CS3 this wasn't possible when applying filters.

What are Smart Filters?

I should start by briefly mentioning Smart Objects. They were introduced with Photoshop CS2, and allow you to import a vector graphic into a Photoshop document as a Smart Object. The object is termed "smart" because it remains fully scalable, just like a normal vector graphic, by maintaining a link to the original file. The natural progression for Photoshop CS3 has been to expand on this functionality by introducing Smart Filters, which provide a fully editable, non-destructive workflow for the application of filters. They're basically adjustment layers for filters, in that they sit above the original image layer but do not irreversibly alter it.

Using Smart Filters

To apply a filter as a Smart Filter, you first need to open an image via Photoshop's standard Open menu as a Smart Object. Don't worry if you forget to do this, or if you already have the image open on your screen, as you can use Convert for Smart Filters under the main Filters menu. You'll notice in the accompanying screen shots that the image's icon in the Layers palette changes to indicate that the layer is a smart object.

All filters subsequently used appear under the image layer as a stack which can be reordered if required, and are applied as part

The image with Smart Filters applied

of a layer mask across the whole image area. You can tell that the whole image will be affected, as the layer mask icon is fully white at this stage. In the example shown here I've applied Gaussian Blur followed by Film Grain to achieve a hazy effect. The small double slider icon to the right of each filter listed in the Layers palette calls up a Blending Options dialog when double-clicked, where the effect of each filter can be adjusted in terms of its opacity, and where each can have an alternative blending mode applied. Remember that, throughout this whole

The original image

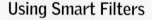

◄ If you forget to open an image as a Smart Object, it can be converted for Smart Filters by way of the main Filter menu.

↑↗ The hazy effect above is achieved by applying Gaussian Blur and Film Grain as Smart Filters. After applying Film Grain I decided the blur effect was a little too pronounced, so lowered the opacity of the filter to 70% by double-clicking on the double slider icon to the right of the filter's name. All filters remain fully editable when applied as Smart Filters.

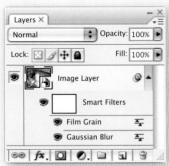

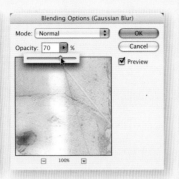

Layer masks

There's another potentially useful technique which you can utilize when using Smart Filters. Areas of the layer mask can be painted out or selected and deleted after the filters have been applied, to reveal the original image beneath. In the final version of the example shown on this spread I've used a black brush to paint out the area of the window frame, removing all filter effects from just that portion of the image in the process.

process, all filters remain fully editable. You can go back at any time and change the settings you've already applied without any further loss of the original digital information contained in the file.

⬆⬈ If you want to remove the effect of the filters from a portion of an image, simply paint over the area with a black brush while the mask is selected. In our example I've painted out the area within the window frame, seen as a black area within the layer mask icon.

Photography: Tony Seddon

119

Resizing images

If you've commissioned photography or are scanning originals for a specific use, the chances are you'll know, at least with close approximation, the planned output size—the size at which the image will be reproduced.

As long as your digital file is the same size or larger than its intended output size, the reproduction quality won't be compromised. Do bear in mind that using images at a resolution much higher than necessary for repro-quality output is not good practice. I discussed image size and its relationship with resolution on pages 098–099, so refer back for specific examples.

There will inevitably be times when you want to use an original image that isn't large enough, and if it's absolutely right in all other respects you've got a problem on your hands. Designers sometimes fail to account for dimensions versus resolution and make the mistake of assuming that, just because an image is 300ppi, that makes it a high-resolution image regardless of end use. With the exception of a vector graphic (see pages 130–131), any enlargement greater than 100% applied to an image within a layout will correspondingly reduce its resolution. In this sense there's no such thing as a high-resolution image, only the high-resolution *use* of an image. An attempt should always be made to source a larger original first. If that's not a possibility, it's time to consider the viability of enlarging the existing image file, and for this you must be familiar with the workings of Photoshop's Image Size dialog.

▨➡ With all three checkboxes on, images are scaled with proportions constrained and the resolution remains unchanged. To maintain a reciprocal relationship between resolution and size, uncheck Resample Image. Photoshop CS3 now also provides a reminder of the benefits of each available resampling option.

The Image Size dialog

If you're resizing images for on-screen use, use the Pixel Dimensions section of the dialog; for print, use Document Size. Constrain Proportions automatically retains width/height relationship, and Scale Styles ensures layer styles applied to an unflattened image are also resized. If Resample Image is unchecked, the resolution is linked to the physical dimensions and will adjust automatically against other adjusted values. To enlarge images while keeping dimensions and resolution independent of one another, switch Resample Image on.

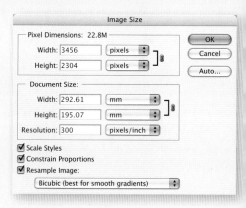

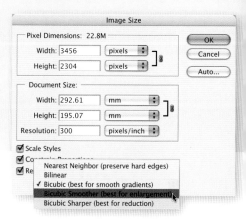

Resampling

When enlarging an image, Photoshop resamples images by analyzing digital information and adding pixels—a process known as interpolation (see page 083). Some would frown on this as a viable option, but if an alternative image isn't available you've no choice. When interpolating, it's important to select the appropriate setting from the drop-down menu next to the checkbox. Avoid the Nearest Neighbor and Bilinear options, as they rarely produce great results. The Bicubic options work by analyzing all eight pixels surrounding each individual pixel, and the results are much better. It's generally best to use Bicubic Smoother for enlargements, Bicubic Sharper for reductions, and Bicubic when you're batch-processing a range of images of various sizes. Photoshop CS3 now provides a helpful reminder of these choices.

Just bear in mind that digital images can't be enlarged without a loss in quality, so take care to judge how much you can afford to lose before the reproduction quality is no longer acceptable.

The original 1488-pixel-wide image reproduced at 100%

Enlargements from a 360-pixel-wide image (left) at 200% and 413%

⬆ Scaling an image up significantly will always result in a loss of quality, particularly when the image contains a lot of detail. The 200% enlargement is already displaying a loss of quality, and the 413% enlargement is completely unacceptable.

Image: iStockphoto.com

TIP

If you really must enlarge an image by a relatively large amount, try doing it gradually in small increments of 1–2% rather than in one hit. It depends on the image, and doesn't always work, but can on occasion produce a better final result.

Sharpening

It's a certainty that digital images, even when captured using high-end devices, will need to be sharpened. Photographers can do this if you specify it as part of their brief, but I prefer to receive images unsharpened.

Because sharpening works by emphasizing the difference, or contrast, between light and dark pixels, pixel values are altered. This makes sharpening a destructive process, so it's best left until the end of the image workflow. I don't sharpen archived originals for this reason.

Basic sharpening

The basic options that appear under the *Filter > Sharpen* menu aren't terribly useful, and I wouldn't recommend them. The problem with these options is that they affect the whole image without providing any control or fine-tuning of the end result. If all you need is a quick result for a visual or something similar, these options are OK, but the next two filters on the menu provide much better choices. Once you understand how they work, I doubt you'll elect to use any of the basic options again.

The Unsharp Mask filter

Also accessed via the *Filter > Sharpen* menu, Photoshop's Unsharp Mask filter provides a sophisticated sharpening tool in the form of three sliders. The Amount setting dictates how much contrast is added between pixels, and therefore determines the strength of the sharpening effect. A high percentage setting in this field will significantly increase the contrast along the visible edges in an image. The Radius setting delineates the area affected by the specified amount of sharpening. One unpleasant result of over-sharpening is the halo effect—a white outline that traces contrasting edges. The Radius slider limits this effect. The Threshold setting dictates how much difference, or contrast, there should be between adjacent pixels before sharpening is applied. If this slider is set to 0, every part of the image will be sharpened. As you increase the threshold value, only contrasting areas will be affected, thus decreasing the sharpening overall.

I follow a standard method for sharpening using Unsharp Mask that works well for most image types. Start with the Amount setting at 250—the midpoint of the slider's range; set Radius at 1, and leave Threshold on 0. With these settings the image probably won't look right—details will be overemphasized, particularly along edges, and the sharpening

 The original image (left) of Willow is quite soft, particularly in the fine detail in her coat and in the grass. The application of the Unsharp Mask filter through two stages produces a marked improvement. Note the relatively low values in the Radius and Threshold fields of the final settings.

Photography: Tony Seddon

won't look at all natural. Next, increase the Threshold setting gradually until any areas of the image displaying too much textured detail begin to smooth out. Follow this by edging the Radius slider up (or down) until the halo effect is as minimal as possible. To produce a pleasing result I find that both these settings normally end up having relatively low values. Finally, reduce the Amount setting until you're happy that the image doesn't appear over-sharpened. The ideal sharpening settings will vary from image to image, so play around with them until you achieve the best possible result. Remember to toggle the Preview button during the sharpening process to make "before" and "after" comparisons. ☒

This image is oversharp and doesn't look natural

Reducing the Amount and increasing the Threshold produces a much more acceptable result

⊙ Sharpening

The original unsharpened image

The Smart Sharpen filter

The Smart Sharpen filter was introduced with Photoshop CS2 and is effectively a more sophisticated version of the Unsharp Mask filter. The familiar Amount and Radius sliders remain, and function in exactly the same way, but the Threshold slider is replaced by a drop-down menu. The Remove Gaussian Blur option produces results identical to Unsharp Mask. Remove Lens Blur will help make halos less prominent, so, if you need to set fairly high values in the Amount and Radius fields to get a satisfactory result, this is a good choice.

Remove Motion Blur reduces the effects of camera shake, but personally I find it quite difficult to judge, and rarely use it, as the results I've managed to achieve never look quite right. You may have more luck with it than me, so give it a try and see how it works out for you.

When set to Advanced mode, the Smart Sharpen filter allows the sharpening you've applied to be adjusted in the shadow and highlight areas. For example, problems in shadow areas have a tendency to become emphasized when sharpened. The Fade slider determines the strength of the previously applied sharpening, the Tonal Width slider controls the range of tones affected, while the Radius slider affects what happens in the areas where shadows and highlights blend with the rest of the image.

And finally, don't forget that you can now apply sharpening using Smart Filters (see pages 118–119), so if your images don't look right when you proof them you can go back and readjust the settings without starting from scratch.

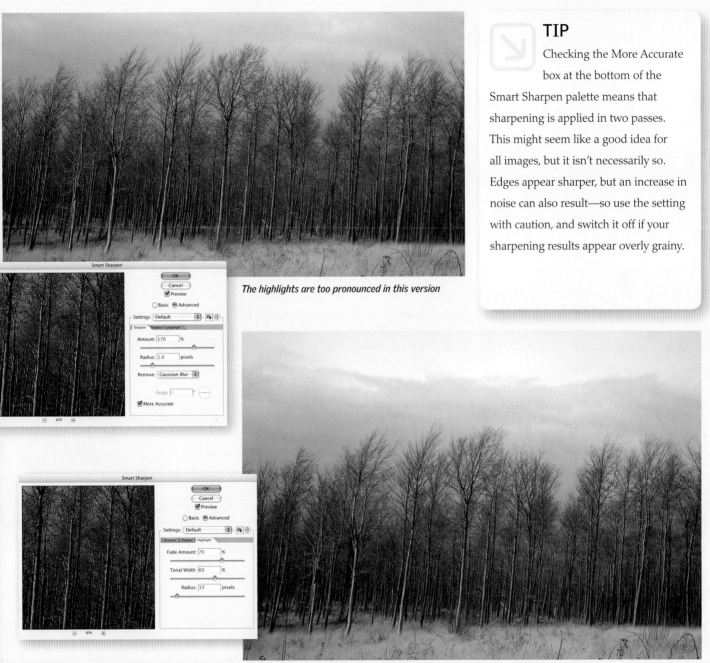

TIP

Checking the More Accurate box at the bottom of the Smart Sharpen palette means that sharpening is applied in two passes. This might seem like a good idea for all images, but it isn't necessarily so. Edges appear sharper, but an increase in noise can also result—so use the setting with caution, and switch it off if your sharpening results appear overly grainy.

The highlights are too pronounced in this version

In this version the highlights are more natural

⬆ Without the ability to adjust the Highlights, it would have been much more difficult to achieve a natural level of sharpness in this detailed image. However, applying the Advanced settings shown in the screen shot has allowed me to fade back the filter's effects on the bright areas of the tree trunks without compromising the detail in other areas of the image.

Photography: Jason Keith

Masking & cutouts

Creating accurate masks or cutouts takes time and a lot of care to get right. Your repro company or printer will certainly be happy to quote for this kind of work, and to be honest it's often a good idea to leave the really complex and time-consuming work to them, but there are occasions when you'll want to do it yourself as part of your own creative process.

Which tool to use?

There are literally dozens of ways to create selections, paths, and masks. The trick is to choose the right tool for the image you're working with, depending on the type of mask you need to create. Here are a couple of practical choices for the kind of masks that you're likely to need as part of a typical workflow you might follow when putting a layout together.

The Pen tool

If you're familiar with the way the Pen tool functions when creating vector graphics in Adobe Illustrator (see pages 130–131), you'll know how this tool works. Clicking along the edge of the area to be masked creates a series of fully adjustable points that can be either corner points or curved anchor points with handles that can be used to alter the curve's path. Click once for a corner point, or click

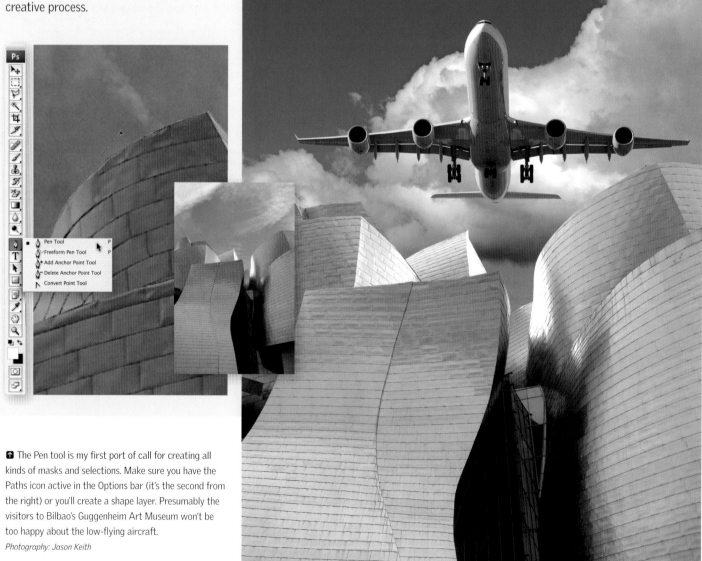

⬆ The Pen tool is my first port of call for creating all kinds of masks and selections. Make sure you have the Paths icon active in the Options bar (it's the second from the right) or you'll create a shape layer. Presumably the visitors to Bilbao's Guggenheim Art Museum won't be too happy about the low-flying aircraft.

Photography: Jason Keith

that have well-defined edges above an evenly colored background. The cursor takes the form of an adjustable round brush with a crosshair at the centre. Click and drag over the areas of an image that you want to remove, and the tool will sample the area directly beneath the crosshair and delete it, leaving a transparent background. The neat part is that you can overlap the areas of the image you want to keep with the brush, but as long as the crosshair is kept away from these areas they won't be removed. Note also that as long as you have the Protect Foreground Color checkbox selected in the

Options bar, whatever color you choose to set as the foreground will never be removed, even if you pass the crosshair over an area containing that color.

The Extract filter

This filter is accessed via *Filter > Extract ...*, and is designed to be used when creating particularly tricky cutouts, such as with fine hair and so on. A highlight tool must be used to define the edges between the background and the foreground areas you wish to keep. Once you're happy that the entire area to be "extracted" has been enclosed, the area ⇨

and drag for a curve point. This tool is best for masks that are made up of smooth curves and straight edges. Once you've familiarized yourself with this tool, I'd bet that making selections with the more basic Polygonal Lasso tool will become a thing of the past.

The Background Eraser

This tool is found in the drop-down menu below the standard Eraser tool and, for me at least, it's one of the most useful tools that Photoshop has to offer when you need to create a cutout quickly. It's great for images

⬆ The Background Eraser is a great choice if you want to remove backgrounds quickly from images with clearly defined edges, such as in this example of an electricity pylon. With a little practice it's possible to achieve impressive results.
Photography: Tony Seddon

↗ Highlighted edges are shown as a green overlay by default in the Extract filter window, with the inner fill shown in blue. Take care to completely enclose the area you want to keep before you apply the Paint Bucket fill, or the whole image will be filled with blue overlay.
Image: iStockphoto.com

⊛ Masking & cutouts

must be filled using the familiar Paint Bucket tool. At this point you can either click the Preview button, or hit OK to save the extracted version of the image complete with a new transparent background. There are additional tools for cleaning up areas and edges if the preview doesn't look quite right, and you can manually extract or replace areas of the image before you commit.

At this point I prefer to save the image as it stands and move on to use another technique for any fine tuning that may be needed. It's quite possible to complete the whole process within the Extract filter window if you wish, but I prefer to switch at this stage to a Layer Mask.

Layer Masks

Layer Masks provide a completely non-destructive method for isolating parts of an image from its background. This is so much better than permanently removing areas which you might want to reinstate when cleaning up edges and when blending cutout images into new backgrounds.

To create a Layer Mask from an image which you've already worked on, for example one that's been manipulated with the Extract filter, first click on the image's thumbnail in the Layers palette, holding either the Command key (Mac) or the Control key (Windows). This will create a selection of the remaining visible areas of the image. If you

now click the Layer Mask icon (second from the left) at the base of the Layers palette, a second thumbnail will appear in the Layers palette, next to the original. The black areas of the thumbnail indicate transparency, the white indicates visible image.

A useful trick once you've created the initial mask is to bring back the deleted areas, allowing maximum flexibility when fine-tuning. You can do this by selecting *Edit > Fill* along with the History pop-up menu, which returns the extracted background to your image while retaining the new Layer Mask. You must do this in the same session as the initial extraction, otherwise the History information is cleared. Alternatively, you can first work on a copy and then import the Layer Mask back to the original untreated image for final editing.

Once you have your mask in place, standard retouching techniques are the order of the day. Make sure you have the mask's thumbnail selected, then use a brush of an appropriate size and setting to remove or replace areas of the mask until you're happy with the results. A black brush adds to the mask, hiding areas of the underlying image; a white brush removes areas of the mask to reveal the original image beneath.

⬆ When previewing in the Extract filter window, it's not always easy to see the results against the chequerboard background. Use the drop-down menu under *Preview > Display* to select an alternative from the presets, or specify your own alternative choice if you prefer. *Image: iStockphoto.com*

⬆⬇ Layer Masks are perfect for fine-tuning areas of images that have already been worked on using another masking technique. With care and some practice it's possible to create very complex masks that would be difficult to achieve using an alternative technique. *Image: iStockphoto.com*

Specialist tools

If you do a lot of masking, you might want to think about a dedicated software option. One of the most impressive I've come across is Fluid Mask (see below) from Vertus (www.vertustech.com), a Photoshop plug-in which provides you with a set of advanced paint tools to produce extremely precise masks from complex images. Using technology that mimics the way our eyes process visual information, it analyzes texture, color, and edge information in order to create masks and blend edges convincingly. A specialist application such as this will pay for itself in the long run, and the quality of your masking will be consistently high.

⬆ Specialist masking software such as Fluid Mask makes the task of isolating objects from their original backgrounds much easier. This example demonstrates how Fluid Mask uses intelligent edge detection to divide an image into specific regions which can subsequently be removed to create an accurate cutout. When assessing and choosing a specialist application of this type, look carefully at the amount of control it allows over its painting and selection tools. Fluid Mask's ability to adjust edge sensitivity and width when detecting its regions is crucial. More complex images will need a higher edge-sensitivity setting then those with a relatively uniform background. Moving the aircraft to our Spanish location required a few additional adjustments, but using Fluid Mask produce a considerable time saving.

Image: iStockphoto.com

Vector graphics

Vector graphics differ from pixel images because of mathematics. In geometry a *primitive* is the simplest form of geometrical path or shape, and complex graphics are built by combining primitives.

Vector graphics use geometrical primitives such as points, lines, curves (known as Bézier curves after the French engineer Pierre Bézier, who first used them in his work designing automobiles), and polygons. All are based upon mathematical equations which calculate points of intersection and shape, thus representing the image. As the images are not composed of pixels, vector graphic files can be enlarged as much as required without the loss of resolution you would experience with bitmap images. The paths between points are recalculated using the equations, and the graphic re-forms at its new size.

Vector files are generally much smaller in size too. This becomes most evident when images need to be reproduced in print at

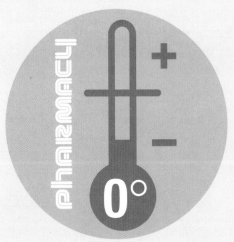

➲ Vector graphics software is ideal for visualizing projects where 3D mock-ups are not available or where real environments don't yet exist, and the combination of vector graphics with pixel art can also provide extremely effective visual solutions. This retail space for technical sportswear brand Pharmacy demonstrates the technique to good effect.
Design: Absolute Zero°

large sizes. Take, for example, the logotype of publishers RotoVision, shown left. The original artwork, drawn using Adobe Illustrator at a width of 100mm, generates an EPS with a file size of only 324KB. When converted to a 300ppi TIFF using Adobe Photoshop, the file size grows to a whopping 6.8MB, which is 21 times larger. The vector artwork is more memory-efficient, and so, produces faster printing through a Postscript-enabled printer.

The main disadvantage of vector artwork is its inability to produce the same degree of tonal gradation and subtle colour shifts that a bitmap image can provide. Therefore, vector artwork is better suited to images composed of flat areas of colour and with strongly defined geometric qualities. However, if photorealism is not what you're after, complex images that utilize vectors can be used to great visual effect. The much improved Auto-Trace functionality provided by vector-based applications such as Illustrator can trace a full-color bitmap, resulting in an image that can be greatly enlarged without any loss of quality.

TIP

If InDesign happens to be your layout software of choice, you can copy and paste vector artwork from a vector-based package such as Illustrator directly into the InDesign page, where it will remain fully editable. Under these circumstances the original vector file will no longer be required for output.

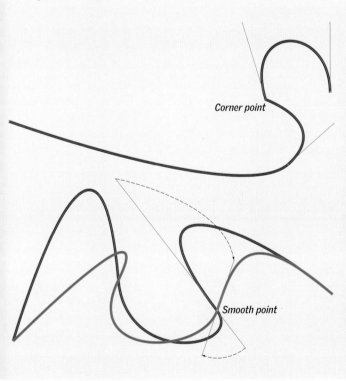

Corner point

Smooth point

⬆ The shapes of Bézier curves are created by moving control handles which extend from anchor points along the curve's length. Anchor points can be either corners (where control handles are not in line), or smooth points (where handles align to make a continuous curve). Note how the positions of the control handles in the lower example affect the curve's shape.

➡ It may look like a rasterized image, but this poster is composed entirely of vector shapes.
Design: My Poor Brain

131

Backing up

People often think of an archive and a backup as one and the same thing, but in fact their functions are quite different. An archive is a permanent copy of data stored for future use. A backup, on the other hand, is a non-permanent copy of data that can be used to restore files in the event of a system or hardware failure, or if files are accidentally deleted or overwritten.

There are some basic principles when it comes to backups that should be considered for all types of digital workflow. Make sure you establish a regular backup routine and that you stick to it rigidly—the use of dedicated software that has the ability to automate the process can help with this. Only back up what you really need, in order to keep the backup file size under control. Again, most dedicated software packages can perform incremental backups that only replace the files that have been worked on since the previous backup, so helping to speed up the process. Finally, consider carefully where you plan to store your backup media, and try to keep a copy off-site for extra security.

Internal & external backups

A set of duplicate files stored on your workstation is known as an "internal" backup. These are useful as a fallback should you accidentally overwrite a file or decide to backtrack on any changes you may have made. However, an internal backup is no use if your computer fails or is stolen. An "external" backup involves saving the duplicate files to another form of storage media such as a CD, DVD, or external hard disk. This is a much safer method to adopt, and I highly recommend that you establish a system of external backups as part of your workflow.

External hard disks

Backing up to CDs or DVDs is perfectly acceptable, but if you back up regularly (as of course you should) you'll end up going through a lot of discs. If you work within a large organization that generates a lot of data, you may well use a form of tape backup. My own preference, however, is portable, high-capacity external hard-disk drives. Such drives are relatively inexpensive nowadays, they can be written to at high speeds using Firewire or USB2 connections, and if they're portable they can be carried off-site at the end of the day. This off-site option is very important. A fire or burglary at your workplace could be disastrous to your

⬆ If your workload merits the investment, you should consider using a server where all your files are stored centrally. Secure RAID (redundant array of independent disks) technology which shares data across multiple disks will provide options for data recovery in the event of a disk failure.

business, but the retention of your digital material will help you to get up and running again quickly. If you can afford it, purchase more than one drive and use them in rotation, allowing you to keep backups that go back further than the previous day.

Specialist software

Windows and Mac users will both find basic backup software built into the standard system configuration, and there are many other packages available from third-party developers. If your backup requirements are complex, however, it's a good idea to research all the available options by downloading trial versions for evaluation; but if you work alone or within a small group, my recommendation is to keep it as simple as possible.

Online backup

Finally, another option is to use an online backup facility, such as that offered by Apple's .mac service. You'll need a fast Internet connection to handle the file sizes involved in the average backup routine, and you may need to purchase additional server space over time, but it's an option worth considering if your requirements aren't too demanding. Remember that most ISPs offer some free online space as part of their standard deal, and again this could be used in your backup plans.

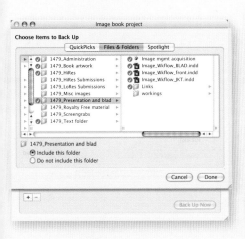

Online backup using a service such as .mac from Apple is an excellent way to store data safely, as long as the file sizes are not excessive. A timed schedule can be set up, and incremental backups which only store changed items will cut down on the time it takes to transfer the data once the first complete backup has been uploaded.

Portable drives like this 500GB model from LaCie are perfect for daily backup routines, as they can be taken off-site overnight for extra security. If you can stretch your budget to two or more drives, they can be rotated, providing you with greater flexibility. This particular model also features biometric (fingerprint) encryption for extra security.

133

The professionals' view

Of all the chapters in this book, this is the most technical. Therefore, it's possibly also the chapter that suggests and outlines working practices which might not conform to many existing creative workflows. I asked a number of designers what procedures they'd put in place, and if they'd ever embarked on complex projects and wished afterward that they'd spent more time devising a workflow.

"We use iView MediaPro to sort and manage images," says Michel Vrána of Black Eye Design. "We create contact sheets which we send to the client for final image selection. The sooner you eliminate images that aren't required, the better it is for the project." Jane Cooper of appliance endorses this view, saying, "We check everything with Bridge as soon as it comes through the door, and then catalog the images we decide to use with iView MediaPro. We also use metadata for larger projects that involve more than a few dozen images, which is particularly useful for us as we operate as a collective with lots of people working from different locations. We post contact sheets online so everyone can reference them during a project."

As to the question of regretting the omission of a more controlled image workflow, most designers admit to allowing one or two projects to slip through the net. "In a number of cases where we've carried out publishing work it would have assisted us greatly to have provided the client with a tighter brief for the supply of images," says Peter Dawson of Grade. "When image quality isn't up to scratch, errors occur and studio time is wasted." Stefan Bucher raises a valid point, saying, "Sometimes big projects don't start out big and you think you can get away with ad-hoc image management. I learned my lesson the hard way many times over, and now I make sure I stick to a coherent filing strategy for each job." He goes on to say,

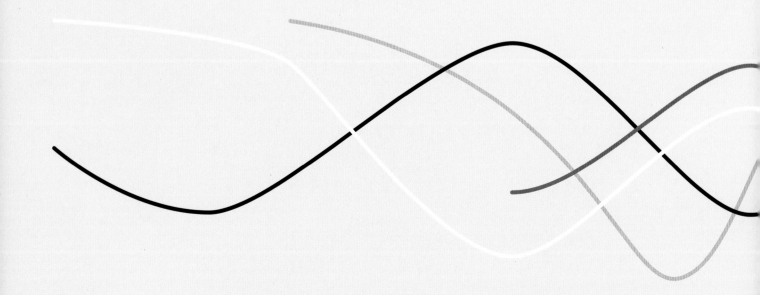

"I want to put as much as I can into making the artwork, so it's important to minimize infrastructure work. I need a system that I can remember, and that's easily explained to suppliers and clients." Russell Hrachovec of compoundEye sums up the benefit of devising an image workflow with, "Anything that prevents us losing or overwriting the time and energy we put into creating an image or design is a good thing, and this sounds awful but it's true: time is money."

I also asked how much responsibility designers are prepared to take over color-managed workflows, image resolution, and basic image quality. The responses were varied, but fell neatly into two specific camps. "Absolutely," says Jonathan Kenyon of Vault 49.

"We calibrate all our monitors fortnightly, and use low-luminance daylight bulbs in the office. Because we work so closely with our photographers, the job of retouching and rendering images often falls within our remit. Paying close attention to image detail, depth, and overall quality ensures we're always working with the best image possible." Tom Morris of Morris and Winrow states, "Anyone producing finished artwork should at least be aware of the issues surrounding image quality. There's usually little or no time for amendments at the end of a job, so all image-related tasks should be resolved before that point is reached." However, many designers find that relying on additional professional expertise for some aspects of the

image-management workflow works better for them. "As a commercial design studio we use a number of different printers, some of them client-appointed. They all have their own requirements for profiling and setup, so we work with them in that respect," says Ian Pape of Fonda. "We do, however, monitor image quality for all projects," he adds. "As designers we all need to understand the technicalities of working with digital image files if we're to liaise properly with repro professionals and printers."

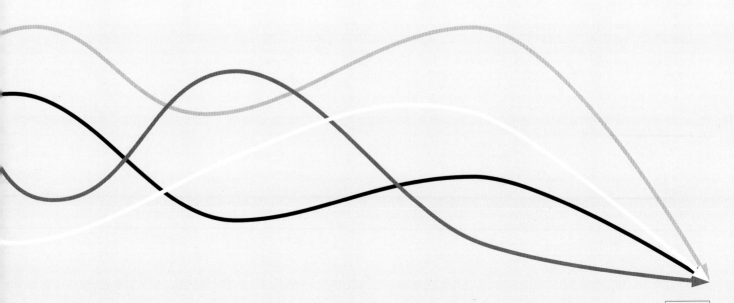

Designing & preparing projects for print

Before everything went digital, it was down to the repro company or the printer to worry about things like resolution, scanning, dots per inch, screen angles, color quality, retouching, and so on. They still do have to concern themselves with these issues, but as designers we must also be aware of the pitfalls that may be encountered along the way. Anything you send to a professional printer will still be thoroughly checked, but if it's in good shape when you send it out you'll soon become your printer's favorite customer.

Images in layouts

Before you work with images in a layout, whether it be for print or for the web, you must be sure you have a clear understanding of resolution. Without this fundamentally important piece of knowledge you can be certain that there'll be troubles ahead.

Bitmap images produced by any digital output device, such as a camera or a scanner, consist of small squares, or pixels, which form a grid. As we've already discussed on pages 096–097, each pixel in an 8-bit color image can be one of a combination of 16.8 million colors. Together the pixels combine to form what looks like a continuous-tone (see Glossary) image with smooth gradations of color and shade, but only if you've used an image of an appropriate resolution.

Pixels per inch (ppi) can only be seen as a relative measure, as the resolution is determined by the number of pixels that make up one inch of an image at its output size. Incidentally, don't confuse ppi with dots per inch (dpi)—the latter relates to the capabilities of the output device rather than the original digital image. Looking at a specific example, let's take an image 6in wide with a resolution of 300ppi, which is the minimum resolution for professional-quality printing. This image will measure 1800 pixels across: 6 x 300 = 1800 pixels. When placed in an InDesign or QuarkXPress layout at 100% of its actual size, it will reproduce at 300ppi. However, if you treble its size to 18in across when you import it into the layout, the resolution will reduce to 100ppi. The direct relationship between pixels per inch and the scale at which an image is reproduced always means that an increase in output size will enlarge the pixels, reducing the resolution and therefore producing a relative reduction in the output quality.

The same applies for images with a low ppi value, but in reverse. I have a camera that records images at 72ppi, but the original image size is large at 3456 x 2304 pixels, or 48 x 32in. If this image is reduced to approximately 11.5in wide it will reproduce at 300ppi, which is the ideal size for high-resolution use in most layout situations. This can also prove useful if, for example, you wish to reproduce a screen

100% / 300ppi

600% / 50ppi

◧⬆ The image on the left is reproduced here at 300ppi and at 100% of its original size. As you would expect, no individual pixels are visible and the image is sharp. When incrementally enlarged "in-layout" to 600%, the effective resolution decreases and the pixels are visible in the right-hand image.

Image: istockphoto.com

grab which in its original form is either 72ppi or 96ppi, depending on the platform (Mac or Windows PC) that produced it. If you reduce a 72ppi image to 24% of its original size on your layout, its relative resolution will be 300ppi. Vector-based images are a different matter, as they are not composed of pixels and therefore don't have a ppi resolution. Vector graphics were covered in detail on pages 126–127. ⊞

Image Size

Pixel Dimensions: 22.8M

Width: 2304 pixels
Height: 3456 pixels

OK
Cancel
Auto...

Document Size:

Width: 32 inches
Height: 48 inches
Resolution: 72 pixels/inch

☐ Scale Styles
☑ Constrain Proportions
☑ Resample Image:
Bicubic (best for smooth gradients)

◀ ⬆ The original image file of this street in Peratellada, Spain, is 72ppi and 32 x 48in. However, reproduced at this size (239.5 x 126mm / 5 x 9½in), the effective resolution is 366ppi. This clearly illustrates why pixels per inch must be considered as a relative measure in relation to output size.

Photography: Tony Seddon

139

⊕ Images in layouts

Preference settings for image display

Image-display preferences are the key to how your documents will appear on screen while you work, and it's well worth taking a look at the settings that control how imported images and color are displayed. Your workstation's specification will dictate the range of choices, so don't expect more than your computer is capable of. The screen grabs shown here reflect the best choices for workstations with standard specifications.

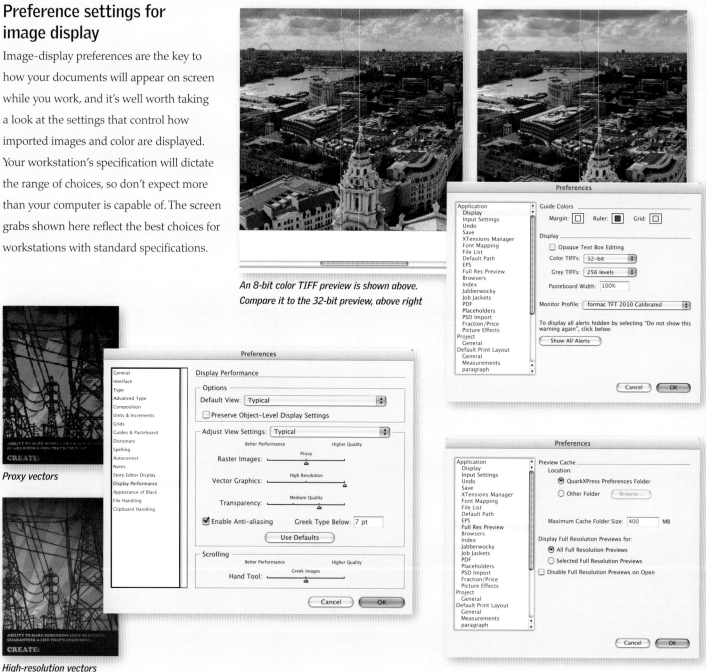

An 8-bit color TIFF preview is shown above. Compare it to the 32-bit preview, above right

Proxy vectors

High-resolution vectors

⬆ The High-quality display option in InDesign is great, but it does slow down screen refresh. I prefer to use the Typical setting for normal working, but with the vector graphics option adjusted to high for better display of imported line artwork. The High-quality display option can be toggled on and off at any time via the *View > Display Performance* menu should you need it.

⬆ The Display settings in QuarkXPress dictate image preview quality for imported images—32-bit for color TIFFs and 256 levels for gray TIFFs creates excellent on-screen previews, but I would recommended setting your preferences to 8-bit for color TIFFs and 16 levels for Gray TIFFs if your workstation doesn't have a high-specification video card installed.

⬆ Quark's Display Full Resolution Previews for setting governs whether images display high-quality previews permanently, or only when the image is selected in the layout. Individual images must be set to full resolution via the *Item > Preview Resolution* menu.

WHITE WINE & SODA

GIN & TONIC

VODKA & ORANGE

TIP

Always ensure that your original images are large enough, in terms of dimensions, to be used at at least 100% when imported into a layout. A 300ppi image is only high res if it is output at an appropriate percentage. Conversely, check that your original images are not overly large. Oversized bitmap images that have to be significantly reduced in a layout produce files that are much larger than necessary without providing a reciprocal increase in image quality.

TIP

Use vector artwork where possible, as when importing logos or diagrams. This form of graphic is not composed of pixels and can be enlarged to any size without a loss of quality. Screen previews may not look too good for enlarged images, but can be improved by using the appropriate display preferences (see opposite), and file sizes are also generally much smaller.

⊟ Vector graphics can be enlarged as much as you want without loss of quality, as they are constructed from lines and curves controlled by mathematical equations. All these logos, designed as part of a student project for a fictional alcoholic sweet product, are placed from the same original .eps file.

Design: My Poor Brain

141

Master pages & layers

Master pages, which can be created in both InDesign and QuarkXPress, are a form of template that dictates which elements of a layout's design appear on every page. The advantages that master pages provide are considerable, but badly constructed master pages can be more trouble than they're worth.

The trick isn't in deciding what to include on them, it's more to do with what has to be subsequently deleted or amended on the document pages. This is particularly relevant when working with images. If an image repeats regularly throughout a document, it's an ideal candidate for inclusion. Think carefully, however, before including images that aren't required on every page. For example, if your pages include a picture frame that is consistently positioned but will contain a different image each time, it's worth including it on the master page, but place it as an empty frame. Don't import an image into the frame on the master page, as you'll only have to replace it in all your subsequent document pages.

InDesign and QuarkXPress deal with master-page objects a little differently. In QuarkXPress, master-page objects are immediately available for editing, or overriding, in document pages. Overriding automatically removes object links, so changes made to the master page object are not reflected in an overridden item, an important consideration if amendments need to be made. In InDesign, master page objects can't be edited in document pages until you've either clicked on the object while holding down Ctrl-Shift (Windows) or Command-Shift (Mac), or have overridden all master-page objects via the layers palette. I tend to include more objects on QuarkXPress master pages than I do with InDesign because of this extra requirement—which is neither an advantage nor a disadvantage. InDesign can import images without the need for an existing content frame to be pre-drawn, so placing objects from scratch is generally a little quicker anyway.

Working with layers

Page layouts have always been prepared using layers. Traditional paste-up utilized overlays for color separations and images. Layers can be hidden, locked to prevent accidental movement of objects, or even designated non-printing. Separate layers can

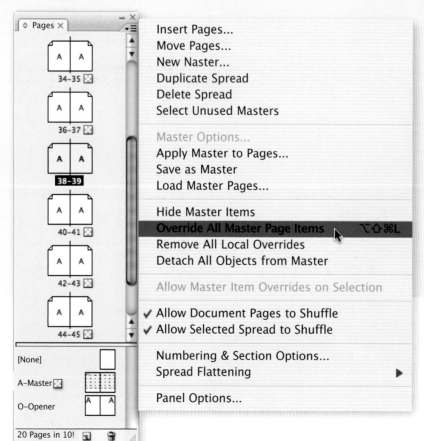

◀ The Page palettes in both InDesign (shown here) and QuarkXPress are very similar in use. In InDesign, Master Page items can be released for editing *en masse* using the Page palette's pop-out menu, where only the selected pages are effected by the action.

be merged, the stacking order can be changed, and layers can be deleted along with all the objects they contain. QuarkXPress even displays a handy prompt when a layer is deleted, asking if you wish to move objects to another layer before they are deleted—a nice touch.

Managing layers

There are a few basic "good-practice" procedures that I've adopted when working with layers. First, don't overdo the number of layers, or documents can become too complicated. Group similar types of material together on individual layers, and utilize the color-coding option to indicate visually which objects belong to which layers.

Second, give the layers proper names rather than the default "layer 1" and so on, and maintain consistency with your chosen naming convention between documents.

Third, use the Lock option to help prevent any "accidental" editing of images. The image layer can be locked or possibly even hidden altogether, helping to speed up the rate at which the screen refreshes as an advantageous side-effect.

Finally, I often create a layer for notes to the repro house and printer. This layer can optionally be deleted before the project is archived.

TIP

If you're producing several versions of a document—for example different options for a brochure cover with alternative images—create a layer for each option. This is also useful for different-language versions of the same publication. That way only one document need be created, rather than multiple versions.

⬆ QuarkXPress requires that a layer named "default" is constantly maintained, so make this the layer that other contributors are most likely to work with. I normally designate this as the text layer, as I always work with an editor on publishing projects.

⬆ It's a good idea to keep the Paste Remembers Layers option checked in InDesign's Layers palette. This ensures that a layer's attributes are retained with an item when it's copied to another document.

A color workflow for layouts

To retain the ability to translate color values accurately throughout an image workflow, you should tag your images in Photoshop (see pages 090–091) with device-dependent color profiles that can be interpreted by color-management software (CMS) built into layout programs such as InDesign and QuarkXPress.

Tagging with profiles is the only way to ensure that CMS will display and output color images consistently across the range of software that you use—so I recommend that you don't leave any images in your workflow untagged. I've already highlighted the importance of building good relationships with suppliers, so if you work regularly with a printer, ask them which profiles they recommend you should use, and get copies of custom profiles they've created for themselves so you can include them in your own color workflow.

Regardless of which software you use, if you keep your color settings synchronized across your entire workflow any images you generate yourself and subsequently import to a layout will utilize the same embedded profiles. Under these circumstances you can decide which profiles to use and then let the CMS do its work behind the scenes without ever having to make any further decisions about color-management policy. However, in

practice many of the images you use will inevitably come from a range of sources and may have various standard or custom profiles embedded, or possibly, won't have any profiles embedded at all.

For RGB images with no profiles embedded I assign the document's default profile, which for me is invariably Adobe RGB (1998), looking out for any resultant color change when applying the profile to ensure the image's color isn't adversely affected. If an alternative profile is already embedded in a supplied RGB image, I tend to convert it to the document default. You'll find that some will disagree with this policy, and suggest that you retain sRGB for images already tagged with this profile. This isn't bad practice as such, particularly if your images are destined for the web or for another on-screen use, but run a couple of tests on a selection of your own images to get a feel for what happens when you assign different profiles, then decide for yourself what looks best for your purposes. Utilize the Proof Setup functionality of InDesign, or Proof Output options in QuarkXPress, to see an accurate representation of your intended output on screen. For supplied CMYK images I generally leave embedded profiles as they are, and follow a "safe" CMYK workflow (see panel opposite). ◗

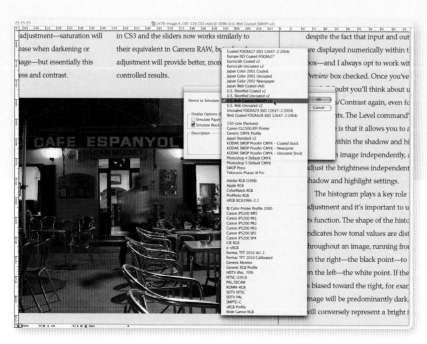

◖ Use Proof Setup in InDesign, accessed via *View > Proof Setup > Custom ...*, to check on screen how the document-wide application of alternative color profiles will affect image color at output.

"Safe" CMYK with InDesign

By default, InDesign supports what Adobe terms a "safe" CMYK workflow. A color settings file is CMYK-safe if the Color Management Policy is set to Preserve Numbers (Ignore Linked Profiles) in the Color Settings dialog. A padlock icon appears next to the CMYK drop-down menu whenever a safe policy is in place. Technically, switching color management off gives a safe CMYK workflow, but because you're not in control of color with that option, I don't recommend it. If you're using a mixed RGB and CMYK workflow with Preserve Numbers (Ignore Linked Profiles), imported RGB images are converted to the document's working CMYK profile when output. If you import any CMYK images that are tagged with a profile that's not the working CMYK

space profile, safe CMYK mode will ignore that profile and preserve the color numbers of those images, thus preventing unexpected color shifts away from what you see on screen. Untagged images will be output using the working CMYK profile. If you've reliable knowledge of the profiles your CMYK images are tagged with, it's not strictly necessary to use a safe CMYK workflow, but if you're receiving and using images tagged with a variety of uncommon or custom profiles, it's a good option to choose. Just make sure you inform anyone else working on your files to use a safe CMYK setting that preserves numbers, or the workflow will break down. Remember, too, to check that Preserve Numbers is selected when printing or exporting to PDF.

Color settings for QuarkXPress 7

QuarkXPress 7 has completely changed the way it implements the CMS, and has introduced a number of improvements. Separate Source Setup and Output Setup dialogs give complete control over color and images throughout the workflow, allowing you to customize settings fully, use "legacy" settings that match previous versions of the software, or simply use the default setting, which should be good for most situations. To follow an equivalent policy to Adobe's "safe" workflow in QuarkXPress 7, you should leave the Color Manage CMYK Sources to CMYK Destinations box found at the bottom of the Edit Source Setup dialog unchecked.

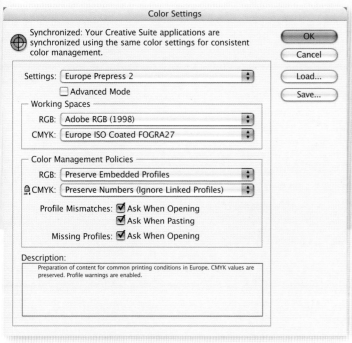

The settings for a "safe" CMYK workflow in InDesign

⬆➡ Separate Source and Output Setup dialogs control image color in QuarkXPress. They're accessed via the *Edit > Color Setups* menu.

⊖ A color workflow for layouts

Working with a mixed RGB & CMYK workflow

Artwork destined for print is normally prepared using the CMYK color model. This approach limits the degree to which unexpected color conversions can occur, and it provides greater control over the appearance of blacks and rich blacks (see Glossary). However, there are compelling reasons for considering the regular use of a mixed RGB and CMYK workflow, particularly with regard to images.

Leaving your images in RGB means they can be repurposed more easily for web projects, or for varying print requirements that may require a return to the original image with its full gamut of color information—remember, the CMYK color space is smaller than RGB. A correctly implemented CMS can accurately display and safely convert RGB images placed in a layout to the CMYK color space without massively unpredictable shifts in color, so what is to all intents and purposes a CMYK workflow can comfortably contain RGB images. Remember, though, as I mentioned at the beginning of this section, it's best to tag all images you use with the appropriate

color profile. If you don't do this, the mixed workflow won't be so successful. Also, make sure your printer is happy to implement the RGB/CMYK workflow, as not all are prepared to do so, and some will charge extra for converting all images to CMYK; and remember to ask them which profiles match their own printing conditions.

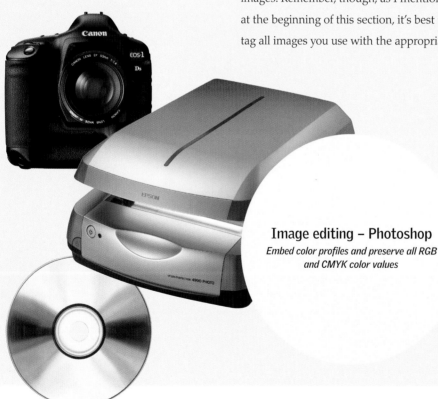

Image editing – Photoshop
Embed color profiles and preserve all RGB and CMYK color values

⬆ The above diagram illustrates a typical mixed RGB and CMYK workflow. Images arrive via an input device, either a camera or a scanner, or from a supplier on CD/DVD. It's also possible that images will have been digitally created from scratch in an application such as Photoshop or Illustrator. Following processing in an image editor, most likely Photoshop, images are proofed on screen or with a digital proofing device such as an inkjet printer. Subsequent design work is carried out with InDesign or QuarkXPress before PDF files are created for despatch to the printer. Color values are preserved during the entire process through the use of color profiles.

RGB content

RGB numbers are converted to the document's CMYK values during printing

Imported pixel and vector images, some with and possibly some without profiles. RGB images with no profiles will use the document profile

 To print

CMYK numbers are preserved during printing

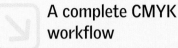 ## CMYK content

A basic mixed RGB/CMYK workflow

A complete CMYK workflow

If you receive images in their original form as color-corrected CMYK files tagged for use under specific printing conditions, there's no point converting them back to RGB for editing. If you really need an RGB original for whatever reason, see if the supplier can organize one for you. Otherwise, use the image as supplied and follow a safe CMYK workflow.

Design work – InDesign or QuarkXPress

Import images as both RGB and CMYK, ensuring the application's color settings are enabled to preserve color values

Export to press-ready PDF

Either convert all RGB to CMYK by choosing PDF/X-1a, or maintain the mixed color workflow by choosing PDF/X-3, which supports both RGB and CMYK

Illustration: Heidelberger Druckmaschinen AG.
© Heidelberger Druckmaschinen AG

⬆⬆ The topmost diagram describes how, by using a safe CMYK workflow, mixed RGB and CMYK content can still be output accurately. All CMYK content uses the document's CMYK profile, RGB content that lacks an embedded profile will use the document's RGB profile, and RGB content with embedded profiles retains its color values through to CMYK conversion.

"In-layout" image adjustment

While many of the standard features of QuarkXPress and InDesign feel fairly similar in use, "in-layout" image manipulation is dealt with quite differently by each package. As part of a suite of individual applications—Adobe Creative Suite (CS)—InDesign integrates with Photoshop and Illustrator for all adjustments. QuarkXPress takes a different approach via the Picture Effects palette, provided by the QuarkVista XTension.

The InDesign solution

InDesign has been engineered to work seamlessly with Photoshop, and in use it does feel as though the two applications are working completely in tandem—but you do of course need to have both applications running. When selected in the layout, an image that requires further modification can be launched directly into Photoshop via the *Edit > Edit Original* menu. The same action can be carried out via the drop-down menu in the Links palette. Once the original image file has opened in Photoshop, adjustments can be carried out (see pages 108–129) and saved (or saved as a new file) on completion. InDesign conveniently updates the imported preview of the image as soon as you move back to InDesign without any need to re-import the file. This is a sensible approach, considering that InDesign is part of the CS suite, and that most designers are familiar with Photoshop's image-editing features.

The QuarkXPress solution

Quark has taken a different approach, which also works well and has a couple of neat implementation features to boot. The QuarkVista XTension, which ships with QuarkXPress 7, provides a Picture Effects palette, accessed via the Window menu. This palette allows familiar image adjustments such as Levels, Curves, Brightness/Contrast, and so on to be applied to a selected image directly in the layout. Furthermore, a selection of filters such as Despeckle, Gaussian Blur, and Unsharp Mask can also be accessed from the same palette. All modifications can be edited at any time,

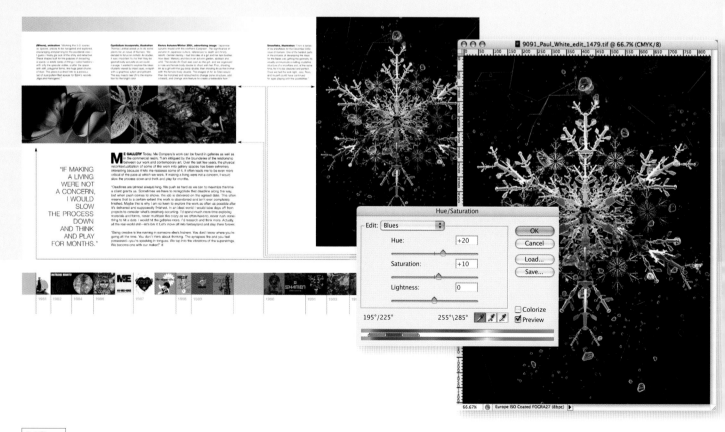

and can be reordered by dragging the items up or down in the palette list. Once the modifications are complete, the final results can either be saved back to the original file, or saved to a new image file via the Picture Export Options palette.

Selected modifications can be switched off at this stage if required, and resolution, color mode, and format can also be changed as part of this export process. There aren't as many options available as there would be while working directly within Photoshop, but those you would expect to utilize for everyday image modifications are here.

To create something new

To share my ideas

Editing an image in InDesign via *Edit > Edit Original* launches the file directly into Photoshop, where all the familiar adjustment tools are available. If you're working on a single image the preview will automatically update when you return to the layout.
Design: Stefan G. Bucher at 344 Design, LLC

The QuarkVista XTension, which ships with QuarkXPress 7, allows image adjustments to be made directly within the layout. The range of available adjustments doesn't extend as far as those offered by Photoshop, but there are enough for all the basic day-to-day requirements.
Design: +Plus with photography by Joe Duggan

Preflight procedures

Before outputting any proofs or film, a good repro company or print bureau will check the supplied layouts carefully—whether they're original layouts or PDFs—and get back to you regarding any problems they encounter with imported images or fonts. However, files should always be checked thoroughly in-house before they're despatched to avoid wasted time and extra repro costs.

At its most basic level, a preflight check involves ensuring that none of the images (or fonts, of course) are missing. Personally I don't regard this as part of a preflight procedure, but simply as part of a well-organized layout procedure. Both InDesign and QuarkXPress automatically prompt you to look for missing images when a document is first opened, so try not to ignore these warnings, and keep images properly linked throughout the entire workflow.

A typical image preflight checklist

The following list represents what I would normally check as part of a preflight procedure, and covers most of the potential image issues for a typical print project. This can all be done using the built-in features available in InDesign and QuarkXPress.

1. File formats & settings

Ask if the repro company or printer has any specific guidelines for formats or preferences, and work with them as closely as you can. For example, they may have their own set of custom color settings that they can supply you with prior to despatch.

2. Imported images

Flag any images that are for position only, or that require additional work such as the creation and application of an accurate clipping path. You can do this on the layout by creating a "notes" layer (see page 143).

⬆ Adding Post-it-style notes to a layout can be very useful, but ensure they stand out enough to avoid forgetting to remove them prior to repro and print. Make sure they're on a separate layer too, so you can show or hide them globally. Finally, use color-coding for different types of note; such as yellow for design, magenta for client, and so on.
Design: Studio Output / Publisher: RotoVision

⬆ InDesign has built-in preflight functionality which, while not extending as far as specialist software, provides all the information you're likely to need when preparing documents for repro and print.

Other important checks should ensure that:

→ there are no duplicated file names;

→ all images are in a suitable format;

→ all images are imported at the correct/optimum resolution and not significantly enlarged or reduced in layout;

→ all images are supplied in CMYK (unless a mixed RGB/CMYK workflow has been implemented);

→ there are no images containing spot colors that will appear incorrectly on a separate plate; and

→ there are no images placed on any hidden layers.

3. Material for scanning

You may be supplying original material in a non-digital format for scanning at the repro house. Ensure that accurate instructions are supplied with each clearly labeled item, and catalog everything in the form of a checklist, which you can refer to when the material is returned along with the first color proofs.

Specialist preflight software

There are several specialist software packages that take preflight procedures to a higher level than those provided by either InDesign or QuarkXpress. FlightCheck Professional from Markzware (www.markzware.com) and Pitstop Professional from Enfocus (www.

enfocus.com) are well regarded, and both companies offer an online preflight product too. This particular kind of service is increasingly popular with publishers and service bureaux now that the Internet can cope with the speeds and file sizes this type of work demands. If you preflight lots of files I recommend that you take a look at one of these products. The huge selection of features will appear daunting at first, but you can customize the settings to report only what you need to know, and the financial outlay will soon justify itself.

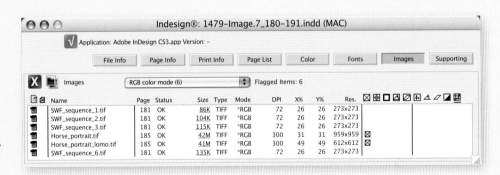

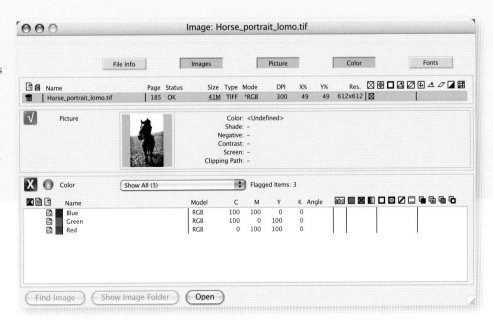

→ Flightcheck Professional can preflight all kinds of files, including PDFs, and offers a huge array of options for checking all aspects of your digital artwork. The screenshots to the right indicate that six images used in the example layout files, made using InDesign, are imported as RGB. Applications such as this go way beyond the built-in preflight options offered by most software packages.

Exporting PDF files

If you use a repro house or print bureau to prepare all prepress material before it is sent to a printer, you're probably still sending out InDesign or QuarkXPress files along with the necessary images and fonts. However, it's now common practice for designers to supply PDF files directly to the printer.

It's another level of responsibility to take on board but, with a little knowledge and through the use of software presets, generating press-ready PDF files is no harder than printing layouts to an ink-jet or laser printer. If you've followed a well-managed digital workflow and are confident that your images are used at the correct resolution and are color-balanced, there's no reason not to implement your own PDF workflow. InDesign CS2 and QuarkXPress 7 both have built-in functionality for generating PDFs that can be utilized for a variety of purposes, and if you use Acrobat 7 Professional you can preflight your own PDF files. Remember, too, that you can still ask your printer to preflight PDFs for you and, if you're going wrong somewhere, advise what you should do to put things right next time.

InDesign presets

InDesign "as installed" includes a number of built-in PDF export presets or job options that are designed to produce PDF files for a specific use. Incidentally, all export presets are also available to the other components of the Creative Suite.

Smallest File Size

This is a good choice for PDFs that will be sent as e-mail attachments for review, or are intended for use in websites. Image quality is low in order to crunch the file size down, so if you want to improve on that, this preset is a good starting point for creating your own modified version (see pages 154–155). By default, all colors are converted to the sRGB color space, which is good for general screen viewing, but be aware that this may result in unwanted color changes for images without embedded profiles that don't match this destination profile.

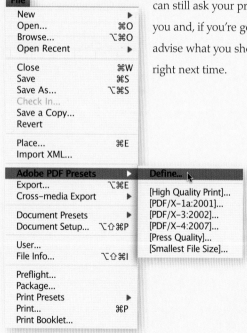

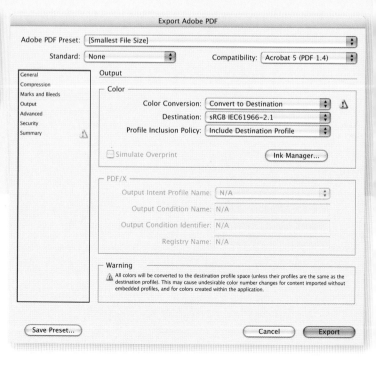

⬆➡ To export a PDF directly from InDesign, select a preset via *File > Adobe PDF Presets*. Custom presets that you create yourself will also appear in this menu. Don't assume that all presets are perfect for all occasions, however. A yellow warning triangle will appear next to any items that could potentially cause problems during output.

High Quality Print

This is a good choice for PDFs destined for output to desktop proofing devices such as ink-jet or color laser printers, and image quality is high. No color conversion is carried out using this default preset, but Tagged Source Profiles are included. This means that device-independent colors are left unchanged and device-dependent colors appear as their nearest possible equivalent in the PDF.

Press Quality

This is the best choice for any prepress workflow that will be output as high-resolution color separations or to a digital press. This option produces a PDF that features "editable transparency," which means that the printers can "flatten" the files later and to their own specification. Colors are converted to CMYK or spot as part of this option.

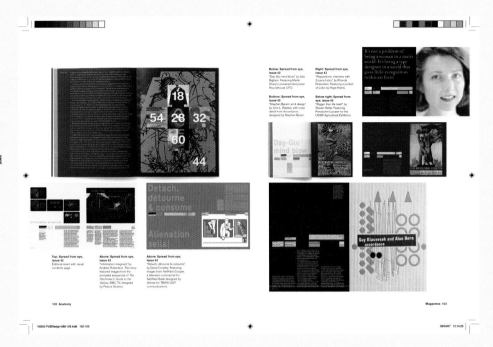

PDF/X-1a:2001

This option is designed for high-resolution output and creates a PDF/X-1a compliant (see panel on page 154) file. All fonts are embedded, color is CMYK or spot, and page boundaries and trapping are defined in the PDF file.

PDF/X3:2002

This option is similar to PDF/X-1a, but it supports a color-managed workflow and allows a profile to be specified for output intent. RGB and LAB colors can be included, which is useful for a mixed RGB/CMYK workflow (see pages 146–147). ⊡

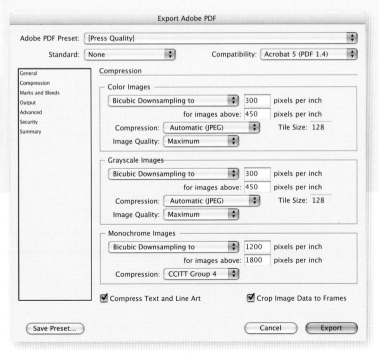

The Press Quality preset will create a PDF suitable for high-end printing requirements, but doesn't take into account any specific standards such as PDF/X. If your printers prefer to handle any flattening themselves, this is a better option than PDF/X. The example above is a press-quality PDF with all printer's marks switched on.

→ Exporting PDF files

What is PDF/X?

PDF/X isn't an alternative format, it's a subset of the Adobe PDF specification. It was designed to help eliminate common problems that occur when PDF files are created—such as missing images and fonts—and to minimize unexpected color reproduction through its support for a color-managed workflow. Using the PDF/X standard ensures your files will be output as you intended. Check with your printer before sending PDF/X files, however. If they prefer to handle the flattening themselves and are highly competent within their own digital workflow, you may get better results using a standard PDF option.

QuarkXPress 7 presets

QuarkXPress 7 ships with just one default PDF preset installed. However, alternative presets that correspond to those described above can be downloaded from Quark's website (www.quark.com/products/xpress/resourcecenter/), and you can of course create custom presets yourself via the Output Styles command (*Edit > Output Styles*), which will be familiar to all seasoned Quark users as its layout is identical to Quark's other Edit dialog boxes. The same principles for PDF generation apply when using QuarkXPress. Image-compression settings, transparency flattening, and color policy dictate how your own custom presets are used.

Creating your own preset

As discussed earlier, you can easily create your own custom options for PDF generation. I recommend beginning by clicking New while an existing preset similar to your needs is selected. This way some of your required settings will be mapped over to your new custom preset.

PDF Preflight

You can preflight PDFs within Acrobat Professional by selecting Preflight ... from the Advanced menu. To begin the process you must select one of the preflight profiles, which include settings for Acrobat/PDF version compatibility, digital printing, PDF analysis, PDF fixups, PDF/A compliance, PDF/X compliance, and prepress.

Once the appropriate profile is selected, clicking the Execute button runs a complete check on the open PDF document, based on the criteria of the chosen profile. It's always a good idea to preflight a document before despatching it to a printer, as the process will pick up things that are very difficult to spot as part of any manual check, such as images used at lower than the minimum recommended resolutions. If you preflight multiple files on a regular basis, consider creating Droplets (see page 185) via the Options menu within the Preflight palette to automate the process.

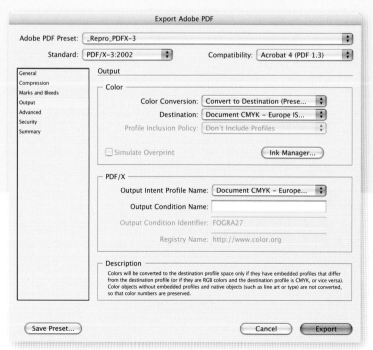

← Creating a custom preset such as the one shown here, which is based on the PDF/X-3 preset, helps to minimize unexpected color changes at output as it supports a color-managed workflow. You can specify an Output Intent Profile, which is normally unavailable for alternative options.

PDFs & images: a best-practice checklist

➲ Always check with the printers to see if they have a preferred PDF export preset, or if they've created their own which they can supply to you for maximum compatibility.

➲ Check also to see if the printer has a custom preflight profile that you can use in Acrobat 7 Professional to check your files before despatch.

➲ When possible, use PDF/X to help guarantee predictable results when your PDFs are reproduced in print, but always check first to make sure your printer can accept the version you've opted to use.

➲ Make sure that all colors are set up correctly, and that there are no unwanted RGB or spot colors, both of which could cause problems with four-color separations.

➲ Take care when placing images in your original layouts, ensuring that their output resolution is sufficient for the intended use of the PDF. An Acrobat preflight procedure will highlight images below a certain resolution, but you'll have to go back to the original layout to rectify the situation.

◄⬆ The results shown in the Preflight palette to the left indicate that the PDF/X-1a compliant file of an earlier page from this book is free of any problems. The preflight functionality is extensive and it's possible to generate a detailed report which can be included as part of the artwork which you send to your printer.

The professionals' view

Preflight procedures have been part of the digital workflow for some time now, especially when it comes to images, and I wanted to find out how much importance other designers placed on this vital aspect of design and artwork production.

Most designers have at least investigated the possibility of integrating specialist preflight software into their workflow, but the majority seem happy with the functionality built into the two main layout applications, Adobe InDesign and QuarkXPress. "I used to use Flightcheck but find that InDesign's Preflight now does everything I need," says David Johnston of Accept and Proceed. "I prep all files using the built-in facility and have never experienced any problems." Michel Vrána of Black Eye Design concurs, saying simply, "We use InDesign's built-in preflight function when packaging a file." Paul Burgess of Loewy sees things a little differently and says, "Our artworking department do use preflight software, but at the end of the day nothing

beats a manual check of everything." This is a view held by other designers I spoke to, as Jane Cooper of appliance confirms.
"We tend to go over layouts twice, once with the built-in preflight function, and once by checking any images that we think may need further attention. It's usually fairly obvious from a visual check which images may not be ready to send to the printers or for PDF generation. If you've got your workflow right to begin with, there shouldn't be any problems, but for a large project there are always one or two images that need sorting out."

Some designers remain committed to relying on their suppliers for preflight requirements. "Personally, I feel that preflight work tips into the domain of the repro

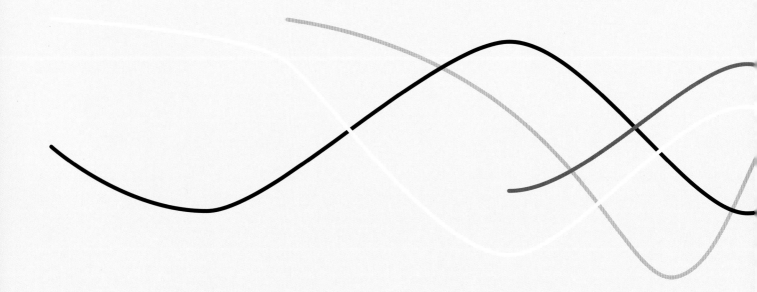

professionals and printers that we work with," says Peter Dawson of Grade. He goes on to answer another of my questions—how do designers prefer to supply finished artwork now that the digital workflow dominates all aspects of artwork production. "We very much prefer to send out collected InDesign or QuarkXPress files. Invariably, due to differing image sources, we end up with a varied mix of media and image quality. This is where the repro guys and printers come in, pulling everything together to create consistency across all the elements."

However, it is apparent that, increasingly, designers who at one time wouldn't have got involved in artwork preparation right up to the production stage, are generating their own PDF files. This can cause frustrations, as Ian Pape of Fonda points out. "We're improving our preflight procedures and practice makes perfect, but it's frustrating when interfaces get reorganized as part of an upgrade, meaning we have to spend time relearning applications." Despite these reservations, Fonda do supply both collected files and PDFs, occasionally both for the same job. "Some jobs may require photo retouching or amendments at proof stage, so the master files must go to the printer. We send press-ready PDF files for our straightforward projects, but for anything more complicated, we occasionally send a PDF and (just in case) include the QuarkXPress files too."

Russell Hrachovec of compoundEye provides a very straightforward response, saying, "We rarely send InDesign or QuarkXPress files to a printer these days. It's pretty much all PDFs now with us." Michel Vrána concurs with this, saying, "We usually provide PDF/X-1a files to our printers. It's a robust file format, and there's no chance of any accidental image substitution." It's obvious from these responses that the constant improvements being made to the prepress functionality of our favorite layout applications will encourage more designers to produce their own press-ready artwork in the future.

Checking & marking image proofs

Compared to some of the other chapters in this book, this one might appear to be rather short. Don't be fooled into thinking its importance has a direct relationship with how much there is to say about the checking of images on color proofs. Learning how to spot problems at proof stage is vital for any designer. This chapter briefly explains what the various types of proof are best for, and how to interpret and comment on color proofs correctly before approving a print job for press.

Proofing methods

Proofing, or more specifically color proofing, is absolutely essential. Checking proofs you've produced yourself in-house before sending a job out is of course important, but not good enough for press approval. You should never allow a job to be printed without seeing some form of proof from the repro house or printer (or both) first.

There are several types of proof in common use today; the type you use will depend on the type of print you're commissioning. Color proofs used throughout a print workflow to maintain accuracy and consistency are known as "contract proofs."

Laser proofs

Lasers are cheap and quick to produce, and can be reasonably representative in terms of color, but shouldn't be regarded as accurate prepress color proofs. The only exception to this is if you're producing a job that's just text and flat tints, or perhaps contains just one or two colors. Under these circumstances you could consider dispensing with the color-proof stage and going straight to press.

When sending material to the repro house or printer for output, I generally supply a laser proof with marked comments which they can refer to when preparing the job for press. Color lasers are better than mono if you have the facility to produce them, and I find that checking a printed laser means I occasionally spot small errors in a layout that I missed during my on-screen prepress procedure. It's also sometimes acceptable for a printer to supply lasers to confirm that a correction has been taken in at a revised proof stage, but only if you've already had sight of a more accurate color proof.

⬆ When you mark up a color proof for amendments, indicate as much as you can with concise notes and suppy an additional set of more detailed notes if they're needed. If it's not easy to add readable notes on the proof itself, write on masking tape. Don't use self-adhesive notes as they will fall off.
Image: Brendan Cahill

➡ If you're printing on plain white stock it's not quite so important to proof on the same stock; just use something close in brightness. However, if you're printing on a colored stock as shown in a couple of the examples here, it's essential that you proof on the same stock in order to see exactly how the color will be affected.
Proofs courtesy of Cahan Associates

Wet proofs

Wet proofs, or "press" proofs as they are sometimes referred to, are the most accurate type of contract proof. They're also the most time-consuming and costly to produce, but if color accuracy between screen and press is critical they're the best option. Wet proofs are produced either on a dedicated proofing press or on the actual press that will be used for the job. Proofing presses are small, flatbed, sheet-fed versions of the larger offset lithography presses, and still require printing plates. These may be the plates that go on to print the actual job, or they may be interim plates produced just for proofing. Either way, if the plates are produced from the same source file using the same plate-making method, the proof will be accurate.

It's worth mentioning that proofs from a proofing press may be slightly less accurate than those from a full-size press. This is mainly due to the fact that large offset presses print ink "wet on wet," whereas the ink is usually allowed to dry between colors on a proofing press. However, if the same ink and paper are used between proof and final job, accuracy should be closely maintained. Proofing presses are used less often now, in line with the increase in jobs produced using computer-to-plate (CTP) technology and digital proofing methods rather than the more traditional film. ▣

Paper stock for proofing

To achieve the maximum degree of accuracy when proofing material, particularly when printing on colored stock, try to ensure that your repro company or printer produces wet proofs on the same stock that the job will ultimately be printed on. At the very least, try to have them use something similar in color and texture. A change in the whiteness, or brightness, of paper can make a big difference to the final color when run on press.

⊖ Proofing methods

Digital proofs

Digital contract proofs, in conjunction with a CTP print workflow (see Glossary), are now generally accepted as the new standard proofing method for high-volume printing. Technically, any digital printer, including your own in-house equipment, is capable of producing an accurate digital color proof as long as it's correctly color-managed. However, for four-color process work, a contract color proof produced by your repro house or printer that is guaranteed to be accurate to their printing conditions is essential. If you've seen and approved a supplied contract proof, and the subsequent printed job doesn't match that proof, it's the printer's responsibility to put things right.

Digital proofs are invariably produced using PDF files generated directly from InDesign or QuarkXPress layouts (see pages 152–155). Eventually the same PDFs will be used to produce the printing plates. It's important that the proofs are made using the press-ready PDFs, as proofs output from the original InDesign or QuarkXPress layouts will not match. Digital proofing devices are essentially sophisticated color-managed ink-jet printers, with some alternative systems utilizing thermal-transfer or dye-sublimation methods. The halftone dots that will eventually produce the color tints on

press are simulated using pixels, which provide a reasonably accurate simulation of how the final print will look.

Digital proofs tend not to be supplied on the paper specified for the final printing. This potential problem can be dealt with via a color-managed workflow, as device-dependent ICC profiles can include information about paper stock and compensate for potential color shifts. However, systems such as the high-end Kodak Approval NX (http://graphics.kodak.com)

can produce digital proofs using CMYK halftone dots on the actual paper stock specified for the job. Spot colors can also be reproduced accurately using a system such as this. However, the initial investment required to install such systems means only large printing firms are in a position to offer this kind of service.

⬆ Large-format digital proofers such as the one shown here are now commonly used to produce accurate full-color proofs for prepress approval. There are several types of digital color proof, normally referred to by the brand of proofing device used, and color accuracy can vary. Always check with your supplier to see what kind of digital proof they intend to provide for each job, and request a sample proof if you're unsure.

Remote proofing

This is still a relatively new method of proofing, and isn't yet as widespread as I think it will eventually become. It's particularly well suited to magazine and book publishing or advertising, where tight deadlines and last-minute changes make this form of "instant" proofing very attractive. Proofing is carried out electronically on a dedicated monitor, which must be calibrated correctly to match a corresponding monitor at the repro house or printers, and no physical proofs are produced. Specially written on-screen software allows corrections to be marked and communicated directly to the repro house or vice versa, or one can simply get on the phone and discuss any requirements in the knowledge that both parties are looking at exactly the same images on screen. Viewing conditions must be carefully controlled, of course, and the cost of high-end equipment and initial setup may be restrictive for small organizations, but the numerous benefits provided by remote proofing are likely to make the method extremely popular in the future. Geographical location will no longer be an issue, and the fact that no physical materials are used to produce proofs makes it ecologically attractive too.

Digital proofing limitations

Spot colors are normally simulated using a CMYK breakdown when part of a digital proof, so are unlikely to appear with absolute accuracy. If you must see accurate spot colors, a wet proof is your best option, but it'll cost extra. Similarly, pure black and white images will be proofed using four-color blacks, so will appear differently to images printed in black only. Once again, a wet proof is the best option if, for example, you're producing a high-quality black and white photography title. Systems such as Kodak Approval NX, mentioned opposite, can produce spot colors accurately but are expensive to install and therefore not always available.

⬆ Remote proofing in use. The example shows an issue of the highly regarded design magazine *Creative Review* during production. Deadlines are always tight on monthly journals such as this, particularly when it comes to the pages containing advertising, so the time-saving aspects of remote proofing offer considerable advantages over other methods.

⊙ Proofing methods

Plotter proofs

These are produced by the printer prior to plate-making, and are used to double-check page positioning and content, not color accuracy. They'll often be trimmed out and collated in book form, and are the final sign-off before a job goes to press. Plotters are normally produced on large-format inkjets, and are the equivalent of blues (or ozalids), which are associated with film-based print workflows.

Scatter proofs

If you don't want to order wet proofs for a complete print job but are keen to see the most accurate color proofs possible for images, consider proofing them separately as scatter proofs. Make up a file with all images placed at the size and crop at which they'll be used in the final job, but economize on the amount of space used by grouping the images together. It may be possible to wet-proof every image in a book or brochure on just a dozen or so sheets. Scatter-proofing is also a useful way of accurately color-proofing images before a layout stage is completed.

TIP

If time and budget are restrictive, consider wet-proofing only selected material that represents a good cross-section of the complete job. For example, if you have a brochure with six sections that each use a different color signature, wet-proof one spread from each section to confirm the chosen colors and tints are working well. The complete job can be proofed digitally, and both sets of proofs can be cross-checked to ascertain the color accuracy of the digital proofs. This won't necessarily save time, and does come with a degree of risk, but it will save on costs.

⊙ Digitally printed plotters provide the final opportunity to check that everything is in the right place before a job goes on press. They're basically color ink-jets printed from the final press-ready PDFs, and have replaced ozalids which were produced from the final film. Plotters are not guaranteed 100% color-accurate, so should not be regarded as color proofs.

Checking color proofs

Most designers will have their own tried and tested procedures for checking color proofs, usually learned by experience. The bottom line is, take time to check every aspect of a color proof thoroughly to guarantee that the final print will live up to your expectations.

It's important to control the lighting conditions as much as possible when checking color proofs. Ideally, you should use a specialized viewing booth with the light source set to 5000 K (kelvins). If this isn't possible, don't use an artificial light source such as a desk lamp—move to a window and check the proofs in daylight. Apart from the obvious things like checking for erroneous marks or blemishes, here are a few specific things to look out for when checking images on contract proofs:

➡ Check the "fit" of all images. This term shouldn't be confused with registration; it refers to the misalignment of color of individual elements, rather than over the whole printed sheet. This is less of an issue now that film is output digitally rather than assembled by hand, and isn't an issue with digital proofs.

➡ Check that registration is correct. Bad registration occurs when one separation doesn't line up with the other, and is only really an issue in wet proofing.

➡ Check that images have been used at a sufficiently high resolution, and that any lo-res positionals used in the layout have been updated correctly with hi-res material.

➡ Check that images haven't been over-sharpened to the extent that they look unnatural, particularly at the edges.

➡ Check that trapping has been implemented correctly and that there are no unwanted gaps between images and adjacent background tints.

➡ Check that there are no moiré patterns (see Glossary) indicating wrongly angled halftone screens.

Color bars

A standardized color bar provides the printer with important information about color, trapping, slurring, and dot gain (see Glossary). Color bars on both the approved proof and the printed sheets can be read by a densitometer to ensure color is matched between the two. The latest printing presses are capable of continuously sampling color-bar information, and will control inking on-press throughout a run to match a preset taken from the original color proof.

◄ The color bars at the side of a color proof provide information about color, trapping, slurring, plate accuracy and registration, and dot gain (see Glossary), and should be manually checked using a magnifier called a linen tester. Modern printing presses can read color bars throughout a print run and automatically make adjustments to the ink flow in order to maintain color consistency during printing.

The professionals' view

I wanted to find out how the group of designers I talked to when compiling these Knowledge spreads felt about proofing methods, as I have my own view of this and was interested to see how many others shared it. It proved to be quite an emotive subject area.

Digital proofs are becoming more accepted as the standard method for proofing full-color jobs now, and many designers are quite happy to go with this. "I think most digital print achieves a very high quality now, and as long as a job doesn't involve special inks or paper it's a very acceptable method of producing color proofs," says Tom Morris of Morris and Winrow. David Johnston of Accept and Proceed agrees with this view, saying, "I'm as confident as one can be with digital proofing and have never experienced any major problems."

Peter Dawson of Grade is equally enthusiastic about the possibilities and advantages provided by digital proofing methods. "I'm very happy with the quality

we get now from digital proofing," he says. "I recently designed a book of photography which was built entirely with high-resolution images supplied directly by the photographer. By ensuring the image workflow was controlled carefully, the absence of any color variation from screen to final print was astonishingly good. I'm happy to pass on press anytime now using digital proofs." It's interesting that Peter still likes to build in a press pass if he's able, as this is always an excellent way to ensure quality in the final print, but do bear in mind that it's not always practically feasible.

Other designers I spoke to took a very different view. "We are not confident at all with the accuracy of digital proofs," says

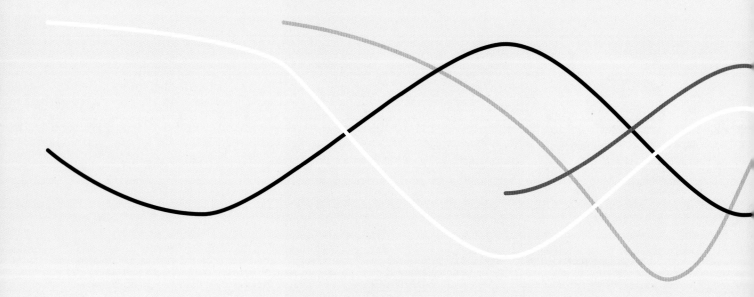

Paul Burgess of Loewy. "Digital proofs tell us very little about how the final job will really look. It's not until you get ink on the paper, and on press, that you see how the job will really look." Stefan Bucher doesn't regard digital proofs that highly either, and states, "CTP (computer-to-plate) is great in many ways, but digital proofs suck! I miss dot-for-dot proofing." Ian Pape of Fonda is cautious of digital proofing but does find something to recommend despite his reservations. "Wet proofing is the best method," he says, "and there is no substitute for ink on paper. However, digital proofs are ideal for checking image crops, the quality of cut-outs, and other various aspects of the layout."

I was also interested to see how extensively the designers used remote proofing methods, and why they might choose to opt for this method under certain circumstances. Time is generally the principal reason, followed by costs. "We still prefer wet proofs," say Sara and Patrick Morrissey of Forever Studio. "However, on a couple of occasions where very late amendments were needed we have approved jobs for press using PDFs." Russell Hrachovec of compoundEye is in favor of proofing on-screen when possible. "It's probably best to never entirely dispense with paper proofs for print jobs," he says, "but I do wish more people would use PDFs or other remote proofing methods as part of their workflow. We often work on repeat

magazine and book projects based on templates we've designed previously, so paper proofs are less important as we can reasonably predict how certain colors will turn out on press."

It would seem that, as digital proofing methods continue to improve, more designers will begin to accept the accuracy of the technique. However, good old-fashioned wet proofs are still the preferred choice for most of us.

167

Designing & preparing online projects

For print designers with little or no experience of designing for the web, the idea of making and successfully publishing a website can seem rather daunting. There appears to be an awful lot to learn, and the software environment and jargon that web designers use differ from those that print designers find familiar. However, web-design applications have seen many improvements in recent years, making it much easier for print designers to make the transition, and when it comes to the images themselves there's a considerable crossover of knowledge. This chapter concentrates on the specifics of preparing and using images in websites, and covers the basics of how to get them online.

Repurposing images for online use

As a designer you're likely to accumulate a sizable image library over time. Much of this material can subsequently be repurposed for use on the web, and potentially even sold on, if the rights remain with you as the creator.

The batch-processing capabilities offered by most image-editing applications should be taken advantage of when repurposing images. Photoshop makes light work of this and provides various optimization presets via its Save for Web & Devices feature. The fact that you can view up to four variations of one file using this system is ideal for ensuring images are optimized correctly. In addition, cataloging software such as Expression Media can produce sets of web-ready images via its built-in conversion functionality (*Action > Convert Image Files ...*).

Because of the limitations imposed by bandwidth for the average Internet user, image size and resolution should always be kept to a minimum if you want your sites to load quickly and smoothly. Don't cut corners when trimming the fat from image files for online use, and don't be tempted to scale images within a site—crop and resize them before uploading to a server. Photoshop's presets are well thought out, but it's still worth experimenting with the settings in the Save for Web & Devices palette. You'll notice from the information displayed in the bottom left-hand corner of each preview pane that even checking the ICC Profile option will increase a file size slightly. Image download times are displayed below the file size and will vary depending on the type of connection speed—for example, JPEG / 60K / 2 sec @ 512 Kbps. Your web images should be considered strictly for screen use only, so, as long as they look good on screen, try to forget the rules that you would follow in a print workflow. If you must provide access to high-resolution images, supply links throughout your site to separate downloadable versions. Remember that although it's possible to repurpose material from print to web, it isn't possible to achieve this in the opposite direction, so be sure to back up your originals.

⬆ Photoshop's Save for Web & Devices palette is an excellent tool for optimizing all images for online use. The two- and four-panel comparison options mean you can visually assess how an image will be affected before choosing which format to use, and the presets provide you with a good place to begin the process.
Photography: Terry Dear

If you're new to working with the web, there are some basic rules you should follow when saving your images for online use. For example, GIFs (Graphic Interchange Files) can be saved with transparency and animated, whereas the photography-friendly JPEG cannot. Vector-based SWFs (Shockwave Flash) are completely scalable and can contain audio and video. File formats occupy an important position in the decision-making process when repurposing images; they are looked at in more detail on pages 176–179.

they are looked at in more detail on pages 176–179.

TIP

Photoshop's Web Photo Gallery (*File > Automate > Web Photo Gallery*) provides an ideal way of repurposing images while simultaneously creating a web gallery based on a preset template. If the gallery isn't quite what you want, it can subsequently be edited using web-authoring software. Dreamweaver, for example, has a clever split-window interface (below) that allows you to view both the layout and the code. Here you can reconstruct the templates to create a more personalized gallery layout.

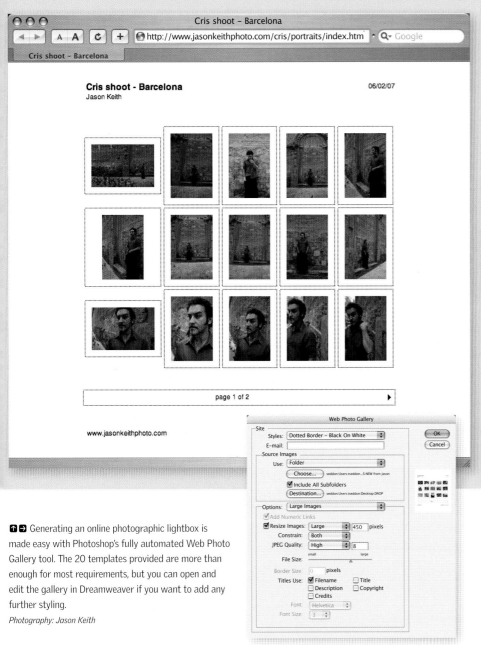

⬆➡ Generating an online photographic lightbox is made easy with Photoshop's fully automated Web Photo Gallery tool. The 20 templates provided are more than enough for most requirements, but you can open and edit the gallery in Dreamweaver if you want to add any further styling.

Photography: Jason Keith

171

Images on the web

If you're approaching the web environment from a print background, there's a lot you can bring with you—and, thanks to its RGB-based foundations, the web offers plenty of scope for using images creatively.

Unfortunately, you may also find that it can sometimes feel rather limiting, as everything revolves around different types of browser. The types and versions used may display your images and layout in different ways. People with low-bandwidth connections may also prefer to browse with images turned off, so it's important that images contain an alt (alternative text) attribute, commonly referred to as an ALT tag. Applications such as Dreamweaver or Freeway allow ALT text to be added easily without the need for additional HTML coding. Incidentally, alt attributes are useful for search-engine optimization, as objects can only be interpreted by analysis of their alt attribute.

As we've already mentioned, image size must be minimized for efficient use of available bandwidth. The constant advances in broadband speed and display technology are making a difference to end-users, but not everyone will have the latest and fastest equipment at their disposal. There may be gaps of several years between kit replacements for Internet cafés, libraries, or government-funded establishments. Therefore, ensure that all images are as highly optimized as possible and are saved using the most appropriate choice of format. Think GIF or PNG for solid-color images and JPEG for photographic material. ⊟

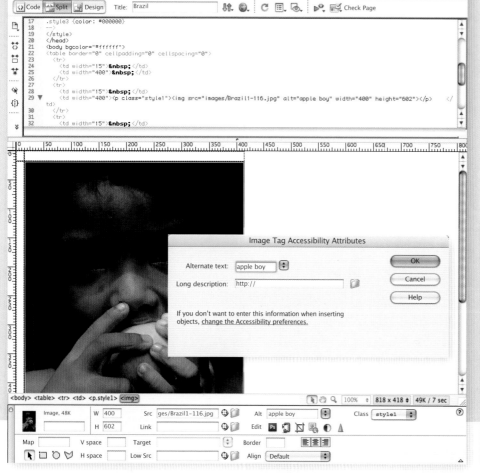

If preferences are set accordingly, the Image Accessibility Attributes palette is opened when you insert an image into a Dreamweaver layout. Enter a brief description in the Alternate text field for each image used, this being the ALT tag. If necessary, enter the location of the file that should be displayed when the original image is clicked in the Long description field. ALT tag text can also be added to a selected image at any time in Dreamweaver's Properties palette.
Image: James Winrow

ALT tag text can be added to a graphic item in a similar fashion while working with Softpress Freeway (see page 175). The relevant field can be found in the Inspector palette.

TIP

Before adding complex graphic content such as animated introductions to a site, think about the increased load time and whether it really adds to the site's value. Offer a bypass link for users with less bandwidth, or produce a Flash version of your website alongside the HTML. Providing options to view a site at different sizes is also a good idea, as long as the design is flexible enough to accommodate this approach.

1024 x 768 pixels

800 x 600 pixels

⬆ Design consultancy Accept & Proceed provide a choice of sizes for viewing their site. Choosing the small option will improve the user experience for those with smaller monitors or less bandwidth.
www.acceptandproceed.com

→ Images on the web

Cascading Style Sheets

It's a good idea to master Cascading Style Sheets (CSS), as they'll give you precise control over your content. It's now a commonly held belief among many web designers that CSS are better for layout work than tables, although in practice tables are still used quite extensively. Using tables can mean that file sizes for individual pages become fairly large because users have to download separate chunks of data for every page they visit, something you can avoid with CSS. CSS also help to make visual consistency easier to maintain across a complete site.

CSS work in a similar way to object style sheets in InDesign. You create a unique data file, either by hand-coding or within your web-authoring application, which contains custom formatting options for specific elements such as images and text, or even a whole page. These can be embedded in a web page or attached via a web-style URL

link. An update to a style sheet applies itself to any other page it's attached to, so content in a multi-page website can be updated in just a few keystrokes. Images can be easily formatted in this way to feature border designs, drop shadows, and other layout-enhancing options that avoid adding to a web-page load time. They also work more reliably across different web browsers and operating systems.

It's perfectly feasible to work with individual images or graphic elements that you've previously created for a print project,

but if you're planning to use groups or combinations of images from an existing print layout it may be better to start afresh with the online layout. InDesign and QuarkXPress can both repurpose layouts for online use, but there's no guarantee of perfect functionality every time. However, web-design applications can lend you a helping hand if any additional optimization of images is needed. Dreamweaver, for example, allows you to select an image on a web page and jump automatically into an image-editing program of your choice. Web-

⬆ Using CSS to add drop shadows to images, in this case while working in Dreamweaver, removes the need to create a separate shadow for every image. Here, each side and all four corners are saved as styles which can be applied universally to every image in a site. If the images change size or shape, the shadow will expand or contract accordingly.

design applications have also harnessed some DTP-like tools and functionality to help print designers make an easier transition to web design. I think Softpress Freeway is a particularly good example of this approach, providing an option that print designers can feel comfortable with thanks to the way in which the application uses a familiar text- and picture-box approach.

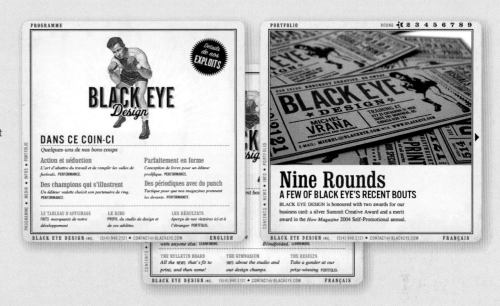

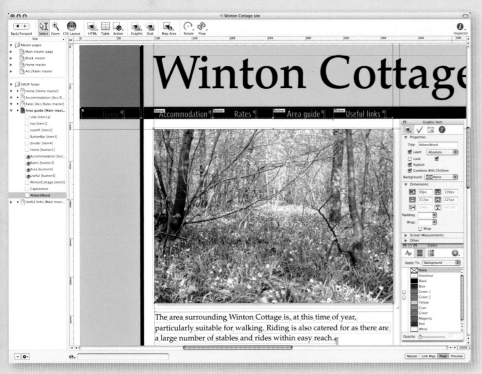

TIP

Pay attention to accessibility issues for visitors with a visual impairment when preparing images for online use. Bookmark the W3C Accessibility Initiative (http://www. w3.org/WAI/) and Jacob Nielsen (http:// www.useit.com/); these sites offer sound advice on the topic and will help you avoid common mistakes.

⬆ Softpress Freeway combines the tools needed for website design with a working environment that will feel familiar to print designers used to working with QuarkXPress or InDesign. The application is a highly automated HTML generator, writing all the code required to display pages online.

⬆ Black Eye Design have used CSS to create a story-based and print-inspired navigation system for their distinctive and memorable website, with a boxing theme derived from the practice name. Their Montreal location requires the site to be instantly available in both English and French, which is dealt with neatly using a permanent link at the bottom right of the screen.
www.blackeye.com

Online image file formats

File formats for online images have remained pretty much the same for some time now. The key formats are GIF, JPEG, and PNG. All are RGB-based and ideal for web use, but each does a different job. These file formats are popular because they offer a good degree of compression—which means everything when working in a web environment.

The Internet, by its very nature, relies on images that have been optimized as much as possible to ensure speedy delivery of content—although faster broadband connection speeds have moved the goal-posts somewhat, and will continue to do so.

GIFs

The GIF (Graphics Interchange Format) has long been popular with web designers due to its compatibility with older browser applications. The format is capable of displaying solid-color graphics with plenty of lossless compression, thanks to a palette of 256 (or fewer) colors, and has extra features including the capacity to create transparent and animated files. GIF images are generally used for solid-color elements such as buttons or logos, as well as for line drawings, cartoons, or grayscale images. GIF images are palette-based, and therefore allow you to reduce the number of colors used. Photoshop allows you to do this manually, or by selecting one of the presets in the Save for Web & Devices palette. This works from a maximum of 256 colors right down to a bare minimum of two, as in black and white images. You'll find that a degree of

32-color GIF with diffusion dither

64-color GIF with diffusion dither

128-color GIF with diffusion dither

◤◤◤ The three images above are all GIFs, but have been saved with varying numbers of colors, resulting in file sizes ranging from 84KB to 108KB. The subtle color gradations are noticeably more stepped in the image with only 32 colors than those in the images with 64 and 128 colors. The color ranges for each image can be seen in their Color Table screen shots.
Photography: Jason Keith

experimentation is required when saving a GIF due to differences between operating systems and browsers. Photoshop allows you to jump between these settings when previewing images in the Save for Web & Devices palette. Other issues that affect the quality of GIF images include the color-reduction algorithm you choose, and the amount of dithering or noise added.

JPEGs

Complex images, such as full-color photographs, are best saved in the JPEG (Joint Photographic Experts Group) format.

The benefits of this format over GIF are immediately obvious: it's much better at displaying smooth gradations in tone and color. The JPEG file format works around mathematical formulas that are controlled by way of a sliding scale when saving images in an image editor. By dispensing with unnecessary data in the file using a "lossy" technique, the JPEG image can be compressed to very high levels without losing too much in terms of color and clarity. Take care when saving, because too much compression in a JPEG will produce telltale artifacts around edges—and there's no way

of putting digital information back in once it's been removed. Both JPEG and GIF files can also be saved so that they appear gradually in a web browser, referred to as "progressive" for the former and "interlaced" for the latter. This does effectively slow the screen refresh rate down by a tiny amount, but transitions are perceived to be smoother because something is always happening on the screen in front of you. ⊟

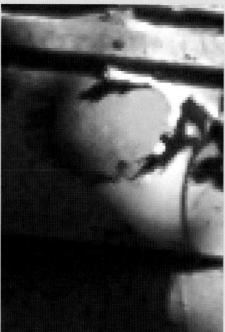
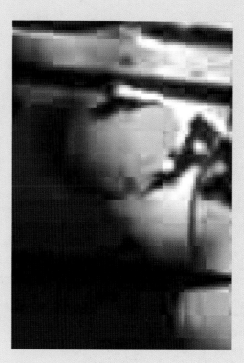

◨ ⬆ ◪ The image to the left is a JPEG saved with the maximum quality option of 12. You have to zoom in to really see the effect of saving this image with a low-quality option. Above, at a 900% enlargement, the pixels are clearly visible. To the right, the large amount of compression has degraded the image quality by a considerable amount.

Photography: Jason Keith

⊖ Online image file formats

PNGs

The PNG (Portable Network Graphic) was devised as an alternative to the GIF file format, and in many ways it offers a more powerful array of features and flexibility over its counterpart. You can certainly do all of the same things with PNG files, such as adding transparency and editing the color-depth details. Perhaps more useful for graphic designers is the fact that PNGs offer a wider range of transparency options than GIFs, including alpha-channel transparency with 254 variable levels rather than just fully

transparent or fully opaque. Furthermore, PNG supports gamma correction to enable cross-platform control of image brightness, and two-dimensional interlacing for progressive display. Finally, PNGs generally compress better than GIFs, but not so much that it makes a huge difference in terms of choosing PNG over GIF. The principal feature that PNG doesn't offer is support for animation, as it was always intended as a single-image format; but this isn't really an issue, as nowadays a large proportion of web animation is created with Adobe Flash.

There are two types of PNG file: PNG-8 and PNG-24. PNG-8 is the best choice for images that you would have saved as a GIF, such as graphics with areas of flat color. Use PNG-24 where you would otherwise elect to use a JPEG. High image quality is achieveable due to the lossless compression associated with PNG, but file sizes can be comparatively large. However, remember that JPEGs don't allow transparency to be used, so if you want to blend an image into a background, use PNG-24.

PNG-24

GIF

⬆ These examples demonstrate clearly the advantage provided by the greater range of transparency options a PNG file offers over a GIF.

⬆ San Francisco design agency Cobra Creative built their entire site in Flash using a series of SWF files. The cinematheque-themed home page features a number of balloons which are animated programatically, following your cursor as you move it around the screen.
www.cobracreative.com

One small word of warning—PNGs aren't supported by some older browsers, so think about the potential end-user for a site before choosing to use PNG files extensively.

SWFs

SWF (Small Web Format or Shockwave Flash) is the proprietary vector-graphic file format produced by Adobe's Flash. Originally a Macromedia application, Flash is an incredibly powerful tool that can be used to produce everything from small graphic animations to complete menu interfaces for DVDs and broadcast television. SWFs are vector-based standalone files that can be highly compressed without loss of detail, and are completely scalable (because they are vector-based), to the point that it's possible to create a full-sized browser window with a Flash-generated SWF file without creating huge files. SWF image files can also contain audio and video footage, and are viewable with the Adobe Flash Player plug-in or standalone player. The fact that the end result is a fully self-contained file with its own links and playback controls means the SWF format is the ideal choice when presenting image slideshows, or when packaging collections of image content, such as portfolios and résumés. SWFs are embedded in web pages in the same way as an image, and work independently from the chosen web-authoring software.

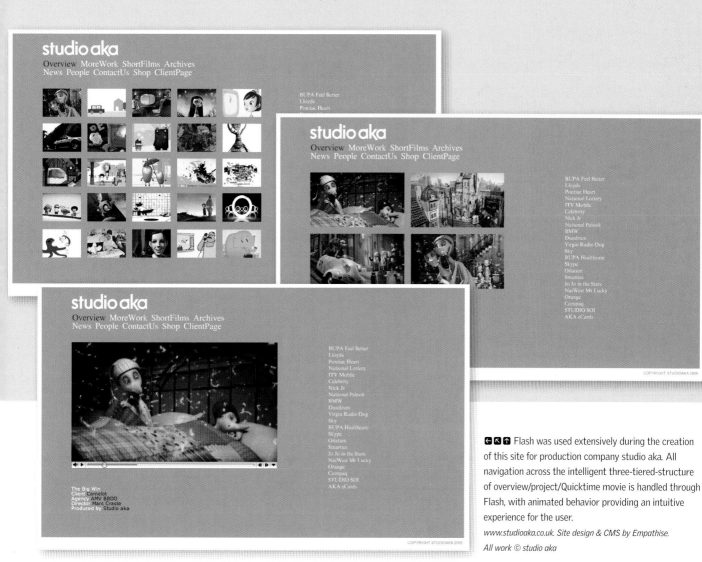

◄ ⬉ ⬆ Flash was used extensively during the creation of this site for production company studio aka. All navigation across the intelligent three-tiered-structure of overview/project/Quicktime movie is handled through Flash, with animated behavior providing an intuitive experience for the user.

www.studioaka.co.uk. Site design & CMS by Empathise. All work © studio aka

Using video online

We've talked a lot about still images throughout this chapter, but you might also need to use a video clip online at some point. Adding video to a site sounds complicated, but in fact it's fairly easy to do, especially if you're using an application like Flash which is designed to keep this kind of thing as simple as possible.

Formats for video

If you're creating an animation from a series of graphic elements or vectors, you'll most likely be using either GIF or SWF formats. However, you'll need to be familiar with different formats when adding video to a site. Video can be downloaded from a link and viewed on- or offline, or it can be "streamed" to a site so it plays while it downloads. The most commonly used streaming formats are RealVideo, AVI, and QuickTime; free helper applications must be downloaded and installed in order to view these formats.

RealVideo (.rm or .ram)

To play RealVideo you'll need to visit www.real.com and download RealPlayer, free. This application will allow you to view near DVD-quality video in a resizable window or in full-screen mode; it can also play QuickTime files.

AVI (.avi)

AVI, or Audio Video Interleave, is a format used commonly for viewing video on PCs. The Windows Media Player is a free download from www.microsoft.com. The format has been around for a while, and considered by some to be a little out of date, but it is widely compatible and is still used extensively.

QuickTime (.qt or .mov)

QuickTime is a very popular video format used throughout the web. The basic Player is free from www.apple.com, and a more fully featured QuickTime Pro license key can be purchased to unlock extra features included in the player application. QuickTime files are particularly suitable for editing due to the separation of individual types of data into separate tracks, or media streams, which are maintained in a hierarchical data structure.

A comparison of RealPlayer (on the left) and QuickTime Player (on the right) reveals the similarities between these two products. Both are capable of producing video playback of a very high quality, as long as the original material is up to scratch, of course.

Embedding video

You can also embed video directly into a web page, which allows you to preset how long the video will play for, and how many loops it will run through. If you're working with an application like Flash, you can import a video clip, such as a QuickTime movie, using the built-in functionality. This means you don't need to worry about setting up an HTML tag for the clip—the application will do all that for you, just as it does with still images.

⬆➡ It's very simple to incorporate a movie clip, such as the QuickTime file used in our example screenshots, into a website while working in an application such as Flash. The movie can be imported directly into its own level via *File>Import>Import Video ...* and embedded prior to the site being published.

Managing online images

Using a Root folder makes a big difference when it comes to keeping images properly managed. Organization is everything, especially as the content expands, and because you'll be working with two versions of the content—the one on your workstation and the version located on a web server.

The root folder

This is a very simple concept and will be familiar to anyone who uses a hierarchy of folders to organize documents. Start by creating a folder on your workstation, the root folder, and label it with your domain name. The root-level folder of your website is the place where your index page, or home page, will be stored on your workstation and on your web server. Inside the root folder, create another folder and name it "images." If you place all images on the website in this folder with relative URL (see Glossary) links, they'll link to the home page or to any other HTML files that you've created in the root folder. That's basically all there is to it. It's a very simple organizational procedure.

Synchronizing & managing content

It's not practical to upload entire websites from scratch every time amendments are made to the content of a site, so it's important to be able to synchronize only the content that has changed. Dreamweaver, for example, has the capability to synchronize website content between your local and online root folders. This is very useful, and offers an array of options to help you decide how your content is moved and stored online. For example, you can opt to move image files and other content to or from your web server, depending on which version of the files is the newest. Before the process takes place, however, there's an added security measure in the form of a dialog window where you can examine all of the files scheduled for modification. This stops you from inadvertently overwriting files. The application also has an area for adding design notes, which can be useful for embedding important information such as when the file was modified, why, and by

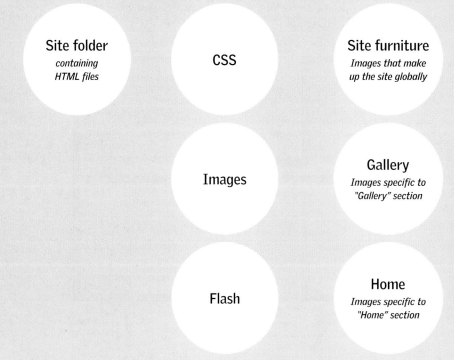

Site folder
containing HTML files

CSS

Site furniture
Images that make up the site globally

Images

Gallery
Images specific to "Gallery" section

Flash

Home
Images specific to "Home" section

⬆ The root folder concept is actually fairly simple and works on a similar basis to organizing images into folders for a print project. In this example, the main images folder that branches from the root contains three further subfolders for images used globally, in a Gallery section, and on the home page.

whom. The check in/check out facility in Dreamweaver also helps to keep files in order, and controls who has access to them.

For simple one-off changes, Adobe Contribute is a stand-alone application that works rather like a scaled-down version of a full web-design package. Contribute allows members of a workgroup to gain access to and quickly update areas of a website. However, they will not be able to make changes to the core structure of the design, only the editable areas of a page as specified by the webmaster. Combining these methods makes it possible to manage images (and of course other types of content) within a website framework quickly and efficiently. Dreamweaver will also ask you if you wish to transfer related files when you alter the structure of a site. In other words, if you want to move a page, the application searches for the images used in that page and moves them too.

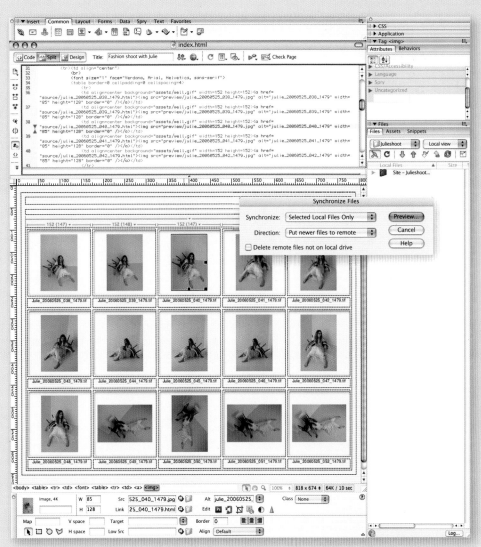

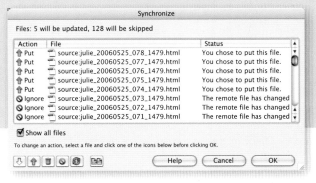

Dreamweaver can synchronize edited content with your remote root folder, uploading just the newer files rather than having to upload the complete site every time you make a change. There's also an additional option to perform a manual synchronization if you know exactly which files have been amended.

183

Scripts, Actions, Extensions & Droplets

The process of managing images in a web-based environment can benefit from a little extra help by way of the automation of certain types of task. This is where the use of Scripts, Actions, Extensions, and Droplets comes into play, all of which allow you to add extra functionality to web pages, or simply speed up workflow by automating repetitive tasks such as batch processing of images.

All four work in different ways, but can transform the way you work. We've touched on how CSS can help control your site's content (see pages 174–175), but Scripts enable you to expand your workflow in many more ways. For example, websites often utilize a feature known as an "array," which is basically a sequence of images played through a repeating loop. These are created using a segment of script which, when inserted into the HTML code for a web page, allows you to show a series of images in a continuous loop. If you want to display large numbers of images without creating lots of separate pages within your site, an array is the perfect solution.

Scripts & Actions

Dreamweaver, for example, has a whole host of scripting snippets that can be inserted into a page as written, or edited to your own requirements via a dedicated palette. Such scripting languages—JavaScript is one of the most common examples—can also be hand-coded from scratch; but if you don't want to spend time learning the technical approach, applications that have these options already built into their interfaces help speed up the workflow considerably. There's also a wealth of Script and Action resources available online—a search on Google will reveal all manner of Scripts and Actions that can be integrated into your project. Implementing them in your own pages is often just a case of copying and pasting the code. This isn't as difficult as it sounds, and web-design applications will make light work of it. Scripts can help to increase the usability of your site, too, by allowing visitors to open new windows to print an image, and so on. Newer web browsers handle this sort of code much more successfully than older versions, and currently Firefox stands as one of the best browsers for producing a consistent and dependable viewing experience.

Graphic designers will already be familiar with Actions, as a number of applications, such as Photoshop and Illustrator, have featured them for a long time, and they too

provide considerable functionality for speeding up workflow. Actions allow you to make a recording of a process in real time, which can then be run to help alleviate the tedium of tasks that need to be carried out regularly.

Extensions & Droplets

There are a considerable number of third-party Extensions and Droplets available for use with Dreamweaver, Flash, and Fireworks, to name a few. These add-ons allow you to boost the power of an application and, in the case of Dreamweaver, there are lots of them—you'll need to install these via the Extensions Manager software that comes as part of the package. Extensions simply require a relaunch in order to become active. Once active, Extensions allow you to add everything from simple image effects through to complex website functionality. Some Extensions are free, and it's well worth spending some time regularly checking out what's newly available for download, as you could save yourself a great deal of time in the long run.

You'll probably be familiar with Droplets if you've been using Photoshop. Droplets are ideal for producing an automated setting for day-to-day chores such as optimizing and compressing images. The Adobe Exchange website (www.adobe.com/cfusion/exchange/

index.cfm) has a searchable area dedicated to Droplets, Actions, Extensions, and a whole lot more besides. Type in your criteria and there will most likely be something that matches. Failing that, Google will soon reveal plenty of third-party sites offering solutions for the same scenario. Be advised though, some work better than others, so test thoroughly before using anything for a live project.

◄ The images displayed by websites should ideally look the same regardless of your choice of browser used to view them. For example, the RotoVision site is working consistently with both Firefox (far left) and Safari.

⬆◄ This great action which emulates the style produced by a Lomo camera is a free download from www.addictedtodesign.com

185

Web-hosting choices

Web hosting is an area that you'll need to acquaint yourself with if you're planning any kind of online presence. Anything that you intend to put on the web will need to have a home on a remote computer, or server, in much the same way as you store images and other files locally, either on your hard disk or on a small computer network.

This also provides a useful way of backing up images and other data into the bargain. Generally speaking, hosting provides the home for a website, and a decent hosting package will allow you to store high-resolution images thanks to evermore generous space allocations and the ability to copy larger data files using FTP.

Anyone with basic requirements may find that the free web space area included as part of their Internet package is sufficient.

The storage quotas for these are generally limited though, and the web URL will invariably be a non-professional-looking address. If you're a designer or illustrator wishing to promote your online presence in a bona fide fashion, the first step is to invest in a unique domain name. This can be done independently, using one of the many online companies providing this particular service. Simply Google "domain registration" to locate a suitable choice.

⬆➡ Opening a .mac account with Apple is an excellent option when getting started with an online presence. As well as providing templates for online image galleries, iDisk gives you an expandable backup and file exchange facility, which is an essential consideration. Additional storage space can be purchased as required and access to your public folder can be password-protected.
www.apple.com

The next step involves choosing a suitable web-hosting package. These come in a variety of shapes and sizes, depending on how much you want to spend, and your requirements. At the very least you'll get a web-space allocation that can often run into several gigabytes. Some packages include online site-building options, which allow you to create basic web pages by working through a series of simple instructions. These are not bespoke, however, so have their limitations—but they can be very useful if, for example, you just need an area that can be used for posting image galleries on the web. Many pro photographers and illustrators who don't feel the need to invest in a completely unique website take advantage of this particular type of site-building service.

Monitoring your site

Once you have a web-hosting package, you'll also be able to monitor traffic to any web page that you build, thanks to site statistics, which measure hits and suchlike. An increasing number of web-hosting packages also offer more sophisticated options, such as adding dynamic content without having to use complex web-authoring programs, providing the capacity for producing web pages that encourage interaction with your audience. These

include popular options such as forums, guestbooks, and customer feedback forms. Again, they are not quite as versatile as coding them from scratch, but work to good effect in the right scenario—especially if you have limited web experience.

→ Once you've decided on a domain name that you like, check that it's actually available, using a site such as UK based 123-reg.co.uk. As you can see, searching for our example domain of designbyappliance.com has revealed that someone (me, actually) has already taken it. Note that I also registered designbyappliance.co.uk, a common practice which prevents others from setting up similar sites with another of the more popular domain endings.

FTP & transferring files

The procedure for using File Transfer Protocol (FTP) for copying images and other files to the web is the last piece of the jigsaw. However, prior to doing this you should carry out some last-minute checks to ensure your files—images in particular—are fully optimized for viewing in a browser.

FTP is essentially a process of copying data to and from a remote server or web host, and there are plenty of software options available. Dedicated applications such as the widely used Fetch or my personal favorite, Transmit, are the best choice, and specialist web-design applications such as Dreamweaver have built-in functionality for uploading files, which make light work of this whole area. To upload using FTP client software you'll need a server address, a username, and a password, along with any other account-specific information needed to reach your web space. Your web-hosting company will be able to supply you with this information if they haven't done so already.

Maintain the hierarchy

One of the main considerations when transferring files is to keep the hierarchical arrangement of your site and its content in exactly the same place after it's copied to the web server. In other words, do not move content into other folders or you're likely to damage the structure of your site. Split-window FTP applications give you the benefit of simultaneously showing files locally and remotely, so you can match them up against each other. Synchronizing them further enhances this. The majority of file, transfer programs will check with you before they proceed to move files to or from a web server anyway. Even if you're dealing with a

⬆ To access a remote server using an FTP application, you will first need to obtain the server address, a username, and a password. Your hosting company, or the administrators of the remote server, will be able to supply this information on request. These details can be saved to a Favorites list once they've been entered for the first time.

large website, the entire copying process should take minutes rather than hours, due to the slimline nature of the content. If it doesn't, then you may have inadvertently left in an oversized image that'll cause a logjam. Stop the process, remove or optimize the problem file, and start again.

And finally ...

I started by saying that this is the last part of the process, but you should also remember that testing online content is the next step that follows on from the upload process. Luckily, Dreamweaver flags up many browser errors or incompatibilities while you're building pages, explains why they have arisen, and duly offers a workaround. Nevertheless, take a look at your images in as many different web browsers as possible, and also across operating systems. You may even spot images that are missing. This occasionally occurs if there are interruptions in your connection or if you've named links or files incorrectly. This is another good reason to ensure that you stick to a dependable naming convention for your files. If you'd care to give them a try, there are online site-optimization services where you can have your pages tested for their efficiency. It's not an exact science though, and there's no substitute for looking at online content in real time to check for errors or omissions.

⬆ Split-window FTP applications allow you to view your local files and folders simultaneously, with the remote server you're logged on to. Transmit features a neat Synchronize functionality that will either automatically update only new files, or completely mirror both sets of material, depending on the settings you choose to apply.

The professionals' view

Knowing that images used in print projects are often subsequently used in online projects that complement printed material, I asked what conversion methods designers favored when repurposing material.

"To achieve continuity between print and web and to develop a consistent brand image for our clients, we're constantly using the same images in print and on the web," says Ian Pape of Fonda. "We've generally found Adobe ImageReady to be the most capable and reliable method for this task." Jane Cooper of appliance adds to this, saying, "We've found that Photoshop's Save for Web & Devices function does everything we need for basic image conversions of this type. We used to use ImageReady quite a lot, as it was convenient and launched straight out of Photoshop, but that's been discontinued now with CS3. We'll probably take a look at Fireworks, which is basically replacing ImageReady. It'll be another application to

learn, but we're told by those in the know that it's worth a look." Stefan Bucher of 344Design has adopted a very simple approach to this. "I repurpose images all the time," he says. "I just resize, up the saturation slightly, and sharpen. That's pretty much it."

I asked photographer Jason Keith how he approached this particular task, as he needs to regularly update his own website in order to maintain the up-to-date online presence which is so important for creative professionals. "I keep complete sets of color-corrected and sharpened images ready for commercial use, which I've processed using my tried and tested methods after each commissioned shoot," he says. "These are always cataloged using iView MediaPro

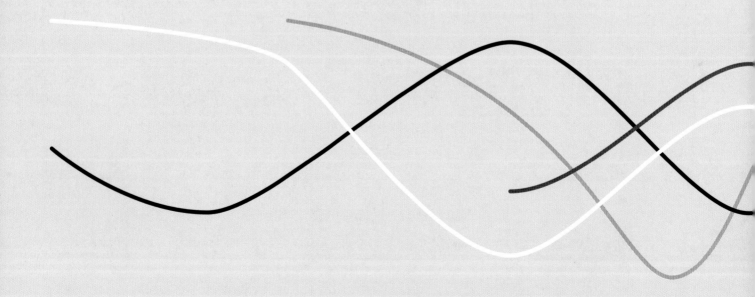

(Microsoft Expression Media from mid-2007) and I use these versions of my images when producing converted sets for the website. As they're already in iView, I often use the built-in Convert Image Files function to produce a duplicate set of images for web use. I like the Save for Web function in Photoshop too. It's very straightforward to use."

I was also interested to know how much importance designers placed on getting involved with image preparation either for their own or for clients' websites, bearing in mind that sites are often designed and constructed by different sets of people. Do they consider the task to be creative or technical? "Well, it's a bit of both really," says Ian Pape of Fonda. "Mostly with us it's a

technical person working under the guidance of a designer, but the designers nearly always get involved in one way or another." Jonathan Kenyon of Vault 49 is adamant that it's a creative task. "We get fully involved," he says, "and we never let any images leave our studio unless they've received our creative input and approval. It's absolutely a creative task." Tom Morris of Winrow and Morris adds to this by saying, "Image quality is so important, and we see their preparation as part of the creative process. Although certain techniques can be applied to a batch of images, the results should still be individually scrutinized to ensure quality is consistent."

It's evident from these responses that designers are generally keen to be as

involved as they can be with the preparation of images for online use. If straightforward batch conversions will suffice, there's no genuine requirement for creative input, but for every other online image-related task, attention to detail and quality will provide considerable benefits.

Archiving & returns

The photography and illustration that you commission, and the artwork that you create with that material, is a valuable asset. It's not necessarily the case that you'll need to go back to every single piece of work that you've ever produced at some later date, but the potential for reusing material that you own the rights to is considerable. It's equally important to take care of non-digital material during the design process, as it may have to go back to the originator.

Archiving digital images & artwork

I touched on the subject of backing up earlier (see pages 132–133), and on the differences between backups and archives. Backups are non-permanent and frequently updated. Archives, on the other hand, are permanent records of data, which should be stored in the safest and securest form possible to ensure they are available for future use.

Any choices you make regarding the type of media you use for your archive and where you store the material should reflect the importance and value of the images—including artwork—that you wish to keep.

Archiving strategy

Like backups, it's a good idea to formulate a strategy for your archiving that includes dual locations. One archive should be located close to hand so it can be accessed easily; the other should be a duplicate archive stored off-site. It's also important to decide how the archive should be structured, depending on the types of project you normally take on and

the average amount of storage space required. My personal preference when working on freelance projects is to make duplicate archives of the final version of every project I complete, keeping all images and layouts in the same standardized hierarchy of folders that I maintain while the project is live. I also never archive different projects to the same disc—every project's archive is self-contained. Sticking to this structure ensures I'll be familiar with the location of all the material on each disc if I need to access it again. One set is kept in a filing cabinet at my house, the other is kept at the studio of a friend of mine alongside

⬆ To keep my remote archive both organized and compact enough to avoid taking up too much space in my friend's studio, I use a relatively cheap flightcase to store each DVD in an indexed hanging sleeve. Periodically I collect the case and update anything that's been amended for a new edition of a book or brochure, thus keeping the archive at a manageable size.

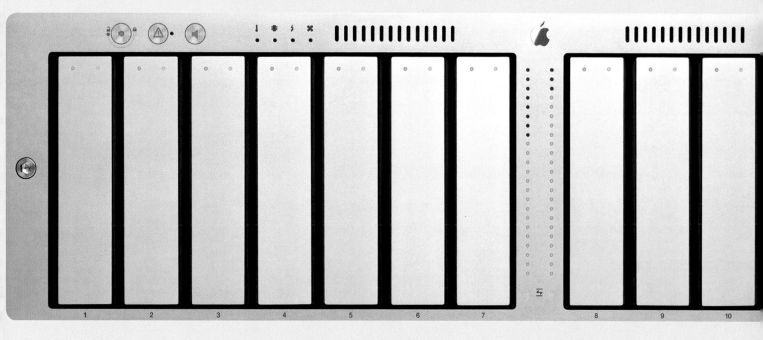

his own archive of design projects. We have a reciprocal arrangement in which I store his duplicate archive, which works well as we each understand the other's system.

If you work in a networked office environment and have access to one or more servers, the options are opened out further. At RotoVision, the publishers of this book, we have a dedicated server used only for archiving completed projects. When a project is sent to repro, all "live" book material is copied to the archive server as an in-house pre-repro archive. It's worth mentioning that before this is done, any miscellaneous or out-of-date material that's no longer essential to

a project is trashed in order to conserve disk space. In addition to this we have an arrangement in place with the repro house we use regularly, whereby all material that goes to press—essentially the "true" archive—is stored by them and forms our off-site archive. A duplicate set of DVDs for each publishing project is sent to us, providing us with an additional in-house archive that includes any extra work the repro house was asked to carry out on images or layouts. Once we've received a project back from repro on DVD and have checked it thoroughly, the pre-repro material on our archive server is deleted in order to

free up space for future projects. It may well be worth speaking with your own repro house or printer to see if they would be prepared to offer a similar arrangement, depending on the type and volume of work you produce. ⊟

⬆ In an ideal world your server will incorporate RAID technology. The term RAID (Redundant Array of Independent Drives) refers to the use of multiple drives which share or replicate data. Benefits include increased data integrity and capacity compared with that offered by a single drive, and nowadays the decrease in drive prices means it's an affordable option for small workgroups as well as large organizations.

⊖ Archiving digital images & artwork

Storage media options

There are various options to consider, based on how much data you regularly need to archive and on how vital your archive is to your business.

External hard drives

As mentioned on pages 124–125, I like to use small external firewire drives for daily backups as they're cheap, convenient to use, and I can carry them off-site easily. They're not such a good choice for secure archiving, however, as they do occasionally fail; but if duplicate sets on separate drives are maintained they can provide a reasonably good long-term storage option.

CD/DVD

CDs are fine for small projects but the larger 4.7GB capacity of standard DVDs makes them the better option of the two for most archiving. Both are fairly stable, last a long time if stored properly away from excessive heat and sunlight, and are relatively cheap. Make sure you purchase the right kind for your equipment, either DVD-R or DVD+R, and stay clear of rewritable DVD-RWs as they're not as reliable for archival use. Manufacturing standards do vary, however, so invest in good-quality brands for peace of mind.

Standardized labeling

This may sound a little excessive, but I have a template for a CD/DVD jewel-case insert which I print out for every disc I archive. It's much easier to search through an archive when all information is standardized and in exactly the same place on each label, and it makes it easier to put discs back in the right place too. Note the inclusion of a master/secondary backup indicator to avoid mixing the two sets.

Job number:

Project:

Burn date:

This is disc [   ] of [   ]

Contents:

This disc is the master/secondary backup *(delete as applicable)*

⬆ Moving beyond the portable hard drive options, there are many excellent large-capacity external hard drive options available. Drives such as these from LaCie are still pretty portable, and can store up to 2 terabytes (2000 gigabytes), so are ideal for larger backup requirements. Make sure a drive has both FireWire and Hi-speed USB connections to maximize compatibility with different workstations.

⬆ This very simple DVD label can be used in a standard jewel case or in a box file with slipcases. Standardizing all labeling means that it's easy to sort through lots of discs when you're searching your archive.

Blu-ray/HD-DVD

The best choice between these new high-capacity formats, designed to replace DVDs, is still difficult to call at the time of writing. Blu-ray discs, backed by Sony, are able to store 25–50GB of data depending on whether they're single- or dual-layer. HD-DVD discs, backed by Toshiba, store slightly less at 15–30GB. Blu-ray would seem to be the better technology, but HD-DVD discs are very similar to conventional DVDs, so manufacturing plants can be adapted for next to no cost. This will, at least initially, help to keep consumer costs down. Either way, both options provide a great solution for archiving, but carry out a little research before buying any dedicated hardware. This will give you an indication of which is out in front as the favored technology. ⮕

Specialist storage equipment

It's worth considering investing in a fireproof cabinet or safe for storing your valuable archive material. Units are normally rated with regard to how long different materials—such as paper or DVDs—stored inside will remain undamaged in the event of a fire, so check this carefully when considering a purchase. Most available options will keep your data safe for at least an hour.

⬆ Check hardware specifications carefully before you commit to a purchase. This DVD burner from LaCie is designed for use with the new Blu-ray discs, as evidenced by the logo on the front of the disc tray.

⊝ Archiving digital images & artwork

Creating an image archive

One of the simplest ways to create an archive which you can be sure contains all the images used in a project is to use the Package command for each separate document (in InDesign), or Collect for Output (in QuarkXPress). You can also save fresh copies of just the images from a document to a separate designated folder. When working with InDesign, use the pop-out menu of the Links palette to access the Copy Link(s) To ... menu item. In QuarkXPress, access the *Save Picture > All Pictures in Layout* ... menu item via the main File menu. This opens an additional panel where further actions such as resampling and color-mode changes can

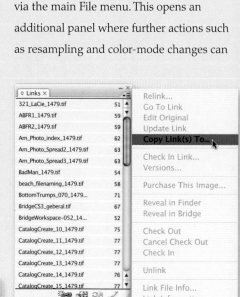

⬆ InDesign (top) and QuarkXPress (above) both have similar features which allow complete documents to be collected together with all linked images plus fonts.

⬆ The Save Picture menu item in QuarkXPress opens in turn an options panel where additional sampling and color-mode conversions can be carried out.

⬆ Images are referred to as "links" in InDesign. If no images are selected in the Links palette, all images in the document will be copied when the Copy Link(s) To ... menu is used.

be carried out—which is a useful function, but at the archiving stage this should already have been finalized. All of these methods will work perfectly well if you've used high-resolution originals throughout the project, but any positionals that you don't want to include in the archive will be copied along with everything else. To discriminate between what you do and don't want to include, return to your asset-management software.

Archiving from catalogs

As part of the cataloging process described in chapter 4, I recommended that you create catalog sets to help isolate subdivisions of images within larger catalogs. These provide the key to the process, as illustrated in the examples shown here which show Expression Media in action.

There are actually two options to choose from with Expression Media, both of which require the Organize button to be selected. You can either select all the images from a particular cataloged folder, as shown in the uppermost screen shot, or you can select a specific Catalog Set. Selecting and transferring or duplicating images in this way avoids copying any unwanted material.

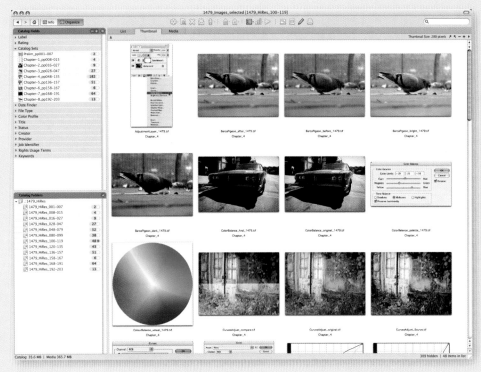

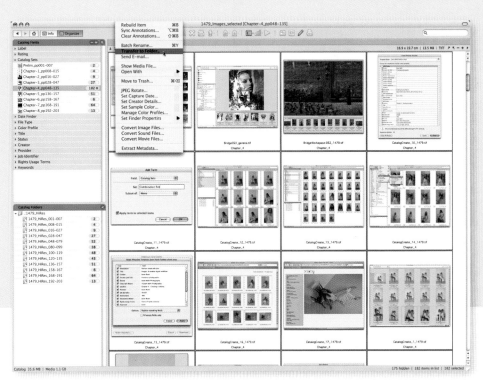

Using the Organize functionality of asset-management software such as Expression Media will help you to create archives at the end of a project which contain all the images used for the final printing.

Original artwork & returns

It would be reasonable to say that the majority of imagery that changes hands today is digital. Previously, when transparencies and flat or reflective artwork was used as standard, valuable original artwork was regularly sent to the repro house or printer instead of high-resolution digital files. This still happens a lot today, despite the domination of digital imagery in most creative workflows.

For example, illustrators who prefer not to work with computers still supply artwork on paper or board. If you don't want to photograph the artwork prior to repro, it must be transported safely and handled carefully, and finally returned to the illustrator once the project is completed. Original artwork normally remains the property of the illustrator, and original transparencies or prints remain the property of the photographer. Originals only become the property of the commissioning party if it's clearly stipulated in the contract or purchase order.

Keeping track

Apart from taking all the necessary precautions to ensure material doesn't get damaged in any way, it's vital that you keep a picture list that identifies clearly which images were supplied as artwork rather than in digital form. The good news is, if you've been practicing good digital asset management with software such as Expression Media or Extensis Portfolio, you've already got your list. Assuming that you're using low-resolution positionals of any artwork that's being sent to the repro house or printer in its original form, those lo-res images can be included as part of your project's image catalog.

There are several ways you can single out the lo-res entries. The simplest is to designate a label as lo-res and apply it to all relevant images included in the catalog. These can then be filtered in the catalog software to produce a list that only includes items that will be sent to repro as non-digital originals. Another way to achieve this is by adding information to a metadata field. For example, you could add "not for repro" to the Status field of all relevant images.

By using the right software tools, you can achieve a great deal with a relatively small amount of effort. A bit of forward planning, combined with a level-headed approach toward the early stages of a project, will pay dividends when it comes to realizing your creative vision.

To allow layouts to progress while high-resolution versions of the images in the Expression Media catalog shown above were sent on DVD from India by the designer, low-resolution versions were e-mailed ahead. It's very simple to single these out in the catalog, because the metadata includes a "not for repro" status note, and a "LoRes positional" label.

Images: UMS Studio, Mumbai

The professionals' view

My final question posed to the creative professionals I spoke to was a simple one. How do you take care of your regular backups and archiving, and do you maintain an off-site archive? Unsurprisingly, everyone had some form of system, with some more sophisticated than others.

"For final archives, we burn two copies per project," says Michel Vrána of Black Eye Design. "An off-site archive is something we are about to implement, just a simple case of one set in the studio and one set at home." This is pretty much all one has to do, and mirrors my own method of keeping a set of DVDs at my friend's studio. "We also have a dedicated backup server that backs up nightly with two alternating sets," adds Vrána. "This way we always have at least a week's worth of backups available."

Ian Pape of Fonda follows a broadly similar method. "A dedicated area of our server is set aside for archiving, and we're currently looking at keeping a duplicate set of files on a remote server for extra security,"

he says. "Each designer also independently backs up daily work onto memory sticks that are carried off-site."

As I've stressed earlier on pages 132–133 and in this chapter, it's essential that some kind of backup, and more importantly archiving, strategy is implemented. Every file that you keep on your workstation or server has a value attached to it, and there's nothing worse than redoing work that you spent valuable chargeable time producing. Remember that you can't charge for it a second time, and clients often return for revised versions or reprints of previous projects. "We archive every night, with off-site storage for all of our workstations," says Peter Dawson of Grade. "It's not at all nice to

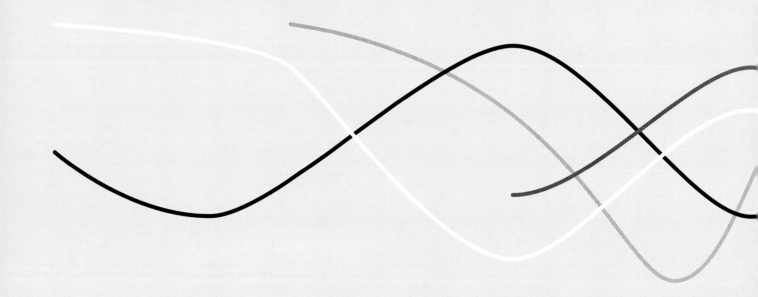

walk into the office in the morning to find empty spaces under the desks where the Macs used to be. Trust me, we've been there! Luckily we were completely backed up and after an emergency shopping trip we were up and running again in five hours."

Jane Cooper of appliance, which operates from several different locations as a design collective, doesn't have the advantage of a dedicated server to which all files can be copied back at the end of each working day. Because of this, members of the collective who are actively involved in live projects copy their files back to a remote FTP server at the end of each working day. "It's not quite as straightforward as a standard studio setup, and is a little unconventional, but it works for us," says Cooper. "As long as everyone sticks to the rules that we've laid down and religiously copies their live files back to the FTP server at the end of the day, it's not that different to a normal studio setup. We use a simple "check in/check out" folder system that doesn't rely on expensive dedicated software, and so far we haven't run into any problems. I back up the working folder to a separate hard drive each day, and if I'm away on vacation the task falls to another member of the collective. When a project is completed it gets archived to duplicate sets of DVDs, and that's pretty much all there is to it."

And that's pretty much all there is to this book, too. I'd like to thank you for reading, and I hope that the methods I've outlined in the last 203 pages will, in one way or another, help you in the formation of your own perfect digital image workflow.

Glossary & reference

Glossary

As this book is about images, the glossary primarily contains entries that relate to the specifics of working with images. However, there are a few entries that I think merit inclusion in any graphic-design related glossary, so they're in here too.

Absolute URL

An absolute URL (uniform resource locator) is a web address leading directly to a specific location or image within a whole website rather than simply within the current page being viewed. The full path to the location always appears as part of an absolute URL. (See also Relative URL.)

Achromatic

A method of color correction employed by color scanners to achieve an extended degree of *undercolor removal (UCR)*. The three process colors generate most color and tone during conventional UCR, with black making up the darker shadows and tones. Achromatic reproduction calculates the very minimum amount of color required, and black is added to give the color its depth.

Additive color mixing

The mixing together of red, green, and blue light in various combinations to create color. Combining all three colors at their maximum value of 255 makes white.

Adobe RGB (1998)

A large, and widely used, color space that includes most of the color gamuts associated with the CMYK color space, plus most other smaller RGB gamuts. It's the best choice when choosing a default RGB working space for documents in a typical print workflow.

Aliasing

Aliasing occurs when a bitmap image has been overenlarged in a layout, or when the original is of an insufficient resolution for its intended use. The square pixels that make up an image become visible to the eye if they're enlarged beyond an acceptable level, and form *jaggies* or visual stair-stepping.

Anti-aliasing

Aliasing can be limited through the use of an anti-aliasing filter. The process introduces additional pixels of intermediate value to jagged edges displaying aliasing, creating a smoother transition between the pixels contained in the original image.

Batch processing

The automatic processing of data using, for example, a script or action. Photoshop actions or droplets are typically used when batch processing images, and can be easily recorded and stored for integration in image workflows. Photoshop has a number of built-in batch-processing functions, accessed via the *File > Automate* and *File > Scripts* menus.

Bitmap

Specifically any image in which each pixel is either on (solid black) or off (white), the result being a monochrome image. However, the term can also be used to describe any type of digital image that is composed of pixels rather than vectors.

Black point

(See White point.)

Blu-ray

A high-capacity DVD disc, backed by Sony, which can store 25–50GB of data depending on whether it's single- or dual-layer.

Camera RAW

A Camera RAW file is the digital equivalent of a film negative. It contains all the raw data recorded by the sensor in a digital camera, as well as all of the camera's settings at the time the photo was taken. Unlike a *JPEG*, a RAW file is not compressed in-camera, so file sizes are larger. Furthermore, as files are not subjected to any in-camera processing, they provide much greater control over the final result. Temperature adjustments (for *white balance*), tint, exposure, and a whole range of additional parameters can be set at the point at which you first open a RAW image. To open a RAW file you'll need the Camera

RAW plug-in for Photoshop, or a stand-alone application from your camera's manufacturer. The latest version of the Camera RAW plug-in, which ships with CS3, can also open *TIFF* and JPEG image files.

Choke

A trapping technique whereby a lighter-colored surrounding background abutting a darker-colored image or graphic object is expanded inward slightly to create an overlap. (See also Trapping.)

Clipping

When converting an RGB image with a large color gamut to the smaller CMYK color gamut, clipping will occur. Color data which cannot be held within the CMYK color space of choice will be removed. Typically, heavily saturated greens and blues are lost as it's difficult to reproduce these colors in print.

CMYK

CMYK describes colors using percentages of the subtractive primary colors cyan, magenta, and yellow. Mixing 100% of all three colors should theoretically make black, but in practice, due to ink and paper limitation, the result is actually a muddy brown. Therefore, black (which is also referred to as the key, so providing the K in CMYK) is added to the

mix to increase the density of color in images and tints. The color gamut of CMYK is smaller than that of RGB, so images that require any color correction work should be dealt with before a CMYK conversion is carried out.

Color control bar

A strip found along the back edge of a color-proof sheet that consists of a range of color and grayscale measurements to help the press operator maintain accurate color from proof to print, and throughout a print run. Modern printing presses are able to constantly scan the color control bar during printing and automatically adjust ink levels in order to achieve complete color consistency.

Color model or color space

A color model or color space describes the complete range of colors that an output device is capable of either displaying or printing. Importantly, color models are either *device-independent* or *device-dependent*. Device-independent models are essentially more precise when describing any one color as they don't need to reference a specified output device. Such models, *LAB* being a prime example, mimic the way the human eye perceives color. Device-dependent models differ in that they are designed to

→ Glossary

provide the numerical values that allow images to be reproduced consistently by monitors, printers, and printing systems. RGB and CMYK are the most commonly used examples of device-dependent models, appearing as a part of pretty much every image workflow. The colors reproduced on screen or in print using device-dependent models are governed by the characteristics of whatever hardware you utilize. They're limited to the range of colors, known as the *gamut*, that your devices are capable of producing. This does, of course, mean that the colors you see using this type of model are not necessarily "true" colors, but they will be consistent throughout your workflow so long as you don't change your hardware halfway through. Besides, if the true color can't physically be reproduced as part of your final output there's no point in being able to see it in the first place.

Color profile

All input and output devices produce slightly different color results, and color profiles were conceived to help achieve consistent color output between these different devices. A color profile is a file containing data that describes how any one device will behave when it deals with color information. There

are three types of profile—input, display, and output—and they work by representing colors as *device-independent* numerical values.

The images you work with are most likely either RGB or CMYK, both of which are device-dependent color models. They work with *additive* (RGB) and *subtractive* (CMYK) primary colors, where the color values describe directly how much of each primary color makes up the color of each pixel on a computer screen or dot in a printed color image. Profiles work by utilizing a *device-independent* color model such as *LAB*. All input profiles contain a table of comparative values that translates the colors in an image to the device-independent color model, known as the *Profile Connection Space (PCS)*. The values can then be translated back to device-dependent color values via a display or output profile, maintaining color consistency. To retain the ability to translate values accurately throughout an image workflow, images should be saved, or tagged, with the required profiles. Color-management software (CMS) built into applications can interpret the tagged profiles at any point in the workflow.

CTP (computer-to-plate)

The process by which printing plates are manufactured without the use of

intermediary film separations. Data is fed directly from a digital file to the platemaking device.

Continuous tone

Prior to its conversion for standard printing using a *halftone* screen to produce dots, or *dithered* for on-screen use, a photographic image is continuous tone. Gradations of color and shade are completely smooth and don't display banding of any sort. It's sometimes also referred to as contone.

DCS (Desktop Color Separation)

This is an EPS-based format which allows each of the four color separations to be split into individual files. A composite master is also generated, and this can be placed in your layout and linked back to the four separation files. It's not immediately obvious what advantage this provides, but it makes the output process much quicker. The preseparated files don't require any further processing when output to a RIP. DCS can also support clipping paths and is often recommended for duotones or other multichannel ink images. The advantages provided by this format only really relate to CMYK workflows, so DCS files provide little advantage under other circumstances.

DCS 2

The next level of DCS development can incorporate the separated data into a single image file, and also supports a mixture of spot and process colors for both *bitmap* and *vector graphics*.

Device-dependent color space

See Color model.

Device-independent color space

See Color model.

Digital asset management (DAM)

Also known as creative asset management, DAM describes the strategy of managing digital assets collectively and individually in terms of version control, for archiving, and for easy retrieval and reuse.

Dithering

A form of interpolation, dithering simulates colors by creating patterns of dots or pixels using the colors actually available within an existing image. A dithered image will look like a *continuous-tone* image when viewed from a suitable distance.

Dot gain

The result of ink spreading between dots during printing. It's normally expressed as a percentage and varies between differing types of presses. It only really occurs noticeably in mid-tone and shadow areas, as highlight areas contain smaller dots, or indeed no dots at all, so the effect in highlights is visibly negligible.

DPI (dots per inch)

The resolution of printed images are expressed as the number of dots of ink per inch as measured on the actual output. The dpi value is sometimes confused with the resolution of the original digital image file, which should be expressed as *ppi (pixels per inch)*. Images that are enlarged after placement in a design application such as InDesign or QuarkXPress will have a lower dpi than their actual ppi resolution. For example, a 300ppi image that is enlarged to 200% in a layout will reproduce at 150dpi. (See also PPI.)

Duotone

A monochrome image that combines two *halftones* produced from the same original, but with different tonal ranges. When printed a duotone will have a greater tonal range than is possible from single-color reproduction. One color in a duotone is normally black.

EPS (Encapsulated PostScript)

Like *TIFFs*, this format can contain both *bitmap* and *vector* graphics. It's able to support spot colors as well as RGB, CMYK, Indexed Color, and grayscale. EPS has its advantages and disadvantages, but remains a good choice for use in a postscript workflow because it is itself postscript based, meaning that the amount of processing required when a file is sent to a RIP is minimized. One disadvantage worthy of noting here is its lack of support for transparency, meaning that any transparent graphics need to be flattened when the EPS is created, and this doesn't always produce the best-possible workflow. EPS files can also be large, even if they're generated from artwork that is not overly complex, because all of the data is embedded to allow the file to be edited if necessary. Having said that, EPS files do compress well. EPS does support low-resolution picture previews however, so the size of the original files may not detrimentally effect the size of your InDesign or QuarkXPress files.

Gamut

The complete range of colors available within any one color space. Be aware that *RGB* gamuts are larger than *CMYK* gamuts, meaning the full gamut of colors viewable on

⊖ Glossary

screen can't all be reproduced by a CMYK output device. In these instances any colors that fall outside an output device's capabilities are matched as closely as possible by way of color management.

GIF (Graphics Interchange Format)

The GIF has long been popular with web designers due to its compatibility with older browser applications. The format is capable of displaying solid-color graphics with plenty of lossless compression, thanks to a palette of 256 (or fewer) colors, and has extra features including the capacity to create transparent and animated files. GIF images are generally used for solid-color elements such as buttons or logos, as well as for line drawings, cartoons, or grayscale images. GIF images are palette-based, and therefore allow you to reduce the number of colors used. Photoshop allows you to do this manually, or by selecting one of the presets in the Save for Web & Devices palette. This works from a maximum of 256 colors right down to a bare minimum of two, as in black-and-white images. Other issues that affect the quality of GIF images include the color-reduction algorithm you choose, and the amount of *dithering* or noise added. GIF files can be saved so that they appear gradually in a web browser, a process referred to as interlacing.

Halftone

The term used to describe any *continuous-tone* image that has been screened and converted to a series of dots, and then subsequently reproduced by way of a conventional printing process. The larger the halftone dot, the darker the shade of color.

HD-DVD

A type of high-capacity DVD disc, backed by Toshiba, which is able to store 15–30GB of data depending on whether it's single- or dual-layer. HD-DVD discs are very similar to conventional DVDs, so manufacturing processes can easily be adapted to produce this newer type of disc.

Histogram

A graphical representation of an image's tonal values. In Photoshop an image's histogram is visible in the Levels dialog box. The dark tones, or shadows, sit at the far left of the histogram, and the bright tones, or highlights, are at the far right. The taller an individual vertical bar is on the histogram, the more tonal information there is in the image at that particular input level. In general a perfect histogram should resemble a conical shaped mountain with each side extending fully to either end of the horizontal scale.

Indexed color

Images saved in the indexed color mode contain a limited number of up to 256 pre-defined colors, hence the term *indexed*. The color values of existing pixels are matched as closely as possible (using *dithering*) against a color look-up table when an image is converted to indexed color. Indexed color images were widely used during the early days of the Internet when modem connections were much slower, as file sizes are smaller than that of an equivalent *RGB* image. Color is of course not as accurate compared with the original, so bear that in mind when choosing to use this color mode. *GIF* files that are limited to a 256-color palette utilize the indexed color mode.

ICC (International Color Consortium)

The organization that promotes the adoption of, and defines the standards for, cross-platform color-management systems for all digital imaging and reproduction.

Jaggies

The visible *aliasing*, or stair-stepping, effect that appears on *bitmap* images that are of an insufficient resolution for their intended use.

JPEG (Joint Photographic Experts Group)

JPEGs are used extensively in online publishing workflows alongside *GIF* and *PNG*-formatted image files, and can be saved so that they appear gradually in a web browser, a process referred to as progressive. The benefits of this format over GIF are immediately obvious: it's much better at displaying smooth gradations in tone and color. The *JPEG* file format works around mathematical formulae that are controlled by way of a sliding scale when saving images in an image editor. By dispensing with unnecessary data in the file using a lossy technique, the JPEG image can be compressed to very high levels without losing too much in terms of color and clarity. Take care when saving, because too much compression in a JPEG will produce telltale artifacts around edges—and there's no way of putting digital information back in once it's been removed. It's never a good idea to edit and resave JPEG images, as the amount of compression specified is reapplied each time. If an image requires an amendment, you should go back to your uncompressed original and save a fresh copy. Leaving the compression level at zero means JPEG files can be used in a prepress workflow without the associated loss of quality.

LAB

Originally named L*a*b*, but now commonly referred to as LAB, this model is made up of three channels that combine to describe color. The L represents luminosity, the A represents color on an axis from red to green, and the B represents a corresponding blue-to-yellow axis. LAB provides the interchange space that allows programs to display and reproduce color accurately between devices. For example, Photoshop converts *RGB* images to *CMYK* by first moving them to LAB mode. This is because, as well as having a larger gamut than other models, LAB is capable of separating an image's luminance from its color. This provides greater control over tonal and color correction, not just when moving between models, but also when manually color-correcting an image in Photoshop.

PDF (Portable Document Format)

The extremely flexible PDF file format can contain a combination of embedded *bitmaps*, *vector* artwork, and text, and is based on Postscript 3 technology. Full support for transparency is available, and fonts can also be embedded when the PDF is first created, for maximum flexibility in terms of distribution, making the format the most popular choice for any documents that need to be sent to a large number of people working on both the Mac and PC platforms. A free "reader" application available from Adobe, the original creators of the format, makes this possible without the need to own the full version of Adobe Acrobat. InDesign, Photoshop, and QuarkXPress are all capable of exporting documents directly to PDF.

PDF/X

PDF/X isn't an alternative PDF format, it's a subset of the Adobe PDF specification. It was designed to help eliminate common problems that occur when PDF files are created—such as missing images and fonts—and to minimize unexpected color reproduction through its support for a color-managed workflow. Using the PDF/X standard ensures your files will be output as you intended. Check with your printer before sending PDF/X files, however. If they prefer to handle the flattening themselves and are highly competent within their own digital workflow, you may get better results using a standard PDF option.

PNG (Portable Network Graphic)

The PNG format was devised as an alternative to the *GIF* file format, and in many ways it offers a more powerful array

→ Glossary

of features and flexibility over its counterpart. Transparency is supported and color-depth details can be edited, but perhaps more useful for graphic designers is the fact that PNGs offer a wider range of transparency options than GIFs, including alpha-channel transparency with 254 variable levels rather than just fully transparent or fully opaque. Furthermore, PNG supports gamma correction to enable cross-platform control of image brightness, and two-dimensional interlacing for progressive display. Finally, PNGs generally compress better than GIFs, but not so much that it makes a huge difference in terms of choosing PNG over GIF. The principal feature that PNG doesn't offer is support for animation, as it was always intended as a single-image format.

There are two types of PNG file: PNG-8 and PNG-24. PNG-8 is the best choice for images that you would have saved as a GIF, such as graphics with areas of flat color. Use PNG-24 where you would otherwise elect to use a *JPEG*. High image quality is achievable due to the lossless compression associated with PNG, but file sizes can be comparatively large. However, remember that JPEGs don't allow transparency to be used, so if you want to blend an image into a background, use PNG-24.

PPI (Pixels per inch)

The resolution of digital images is expressed as the number of pixels which make up one inch of the image. This should not be confused with *dpi*, which expresses an image's output resolution. Images used in a layout at more than 100% of the original size will have a lower dpi than their original ppi, which will potentially result in poor-quality output. If you wish to use an image in a layout at less than 100%, it's good practice to save a copy of the original image file and reduce the physical size to match the final output size, taking care to check Resample Image in the Image Size palette in order to maintain the image's original resolution. This will keep file sizes down and speed up printing. (See also DPI.)

Primary colors

These are the pure colors from which all other colors can theoretically be mixed. Additionally, primary colors can't be created by mixing any other colors. In printing terms the primary colors are cyan, magenta, and yellow, otherwise known as the *subtractive* primaries. The *additive* primaries, which are the three components of light, are red, green, and blue.

Process colors

These are the four main colors of ink, or pigment, used in full-color printing. The *subtractive* primaries cyan, magenta, and yellow are all process colors. In addition, black ink is used because pure black can't be achieved by mixing the three subtractive primaries—you get a muddy brown color instead. Black is also added to increase the density of color in images and tints.

Profile Connection Space (PCS)

The profile connection space is a *device-independent* color model, such as *LAB*, which translates color information that is passed between *device-dependent* color profiles within a color-managed workflow.

PSD (Photoshop Document)

All applications in the Adobe Creative Suite support the PSD format. QuarkXPress 7 can also handle PSD files without the addition of a separate Xtension. Both flattened and layered PSD files can be used, and layers are preserved when placed in a layout. Layers can even be managed directly on the page using the Object Layer Options palette in InDesign, or the PSD Import palette in QuarkXPress. Transparent alpha channels saved in PSD files can also be used as transparency masks in layouts.

Relative URL

A link that is associated directly with the URL of any current online page. A browser will not search beyond the web page being viewed for a relative URL. (See also Absolute URL.)

RGB

RGB is the model used by all computer displays, and describes color as emitted light. Each pixel in each of the three separate red, green, and blue (hence RGB) channels of an RGB digital image is valued on a scale ranging from 0 to 255. The *additive* primary colors (see Additive & subtracting mixing panel on page 087) of red, green, and blue are mixed with differing values to create different colors. When all three colors are mixed at their maximum value (255) they produce white. At their minimum value (0) the three colors create black. On a 24-bit display, 16,777,216 (256 x 256 x 256) discrete combinations of hue, saturation, and luminosity can theoretically be created. In practice, fewer distinct colors are actually produced, but still many more than the human eye is able to detect. For screen-based projects, there's no need to leave the RGB model.

Rich black

To create a denser black, a percentage (or percentages) of other process colors can be mixed with solid black to produce rich black. There are several recognized combinations typically used, one being 86% cyan, 85% magenta, 79% yellow, and 100% black. This unusual combination is derived from Photoshop's *CMYK* equivalent to *RGB* black (0% red, 0% blue, 0% green). Simpler combinations add 60% cyan for a cool rich black or 60% magenta for a warm rich black. Rich black can also be used to help avoid *trapping* issues where, for example, solid black type appears above a full-color image or colored background.

Saturation

This is the term used to describe the variation in color of one distinct tonal brightness. A color that is 0% saturated appears gray, while a color that is 100% saturated is completely pure with no gray at all. For a practical demonstration of saturation, take any full-color image and open the Hue/Saturation palette in Photoshop. If you adjust the saturation slider by moving it to the left, overall saturation is gradually reduced, and eventually the image will look as though it's been converted to a grayscale *bitmap*. In fact the image has been desaturated and remains in its original color model. Bear in mind that, unless you've used an adjustment layer, you can't add destaurated color back later.

Scanner

In graphic design, any one of three main types of device that are used to convert an image, object, or document into a digital file. Flatbed scanners are arguably the most widely used, and incorporate a flat glass plate with a lid-mounted lamp and CCD-type scanning head below. Some flatbed models also feature a separate tray in the body of the unit for scanning transparencies, which can give better results as the glass isn't between the scanning head and the transparency. I've also used a flatbed to scan objects to incorporate into illustrations in the past—the results can be quite interesting.

Film scanners are small units designed to scan only transparencies, and can produce results of a very high quality. They're restricted to certain formats which limits their usefulness in a general studio set-up, but are ideal for photographers who favor one or two specific formats and sell their images in digital form.

Drum scanners are large, expensive devices and are not widely used outside of the reprographics industry because of this. Originals are fixed to a transparent, spinning drum and scanned with a single laser or light sensor. Quality is very high as drum scanners can achieve much higher sampling rates than flatbeds, and their dynamic range, which

→ Glossary

governs how much detail is recorded in shadow and highlight areas of an image, is high compared with other types of device.

Screen ruling (or frequency)

The measure of the fineness of the dots used to reproduce a *halftone* image or a color tint, expressed in lines per inch (lpi). Screen ruling should not be confused with *ppi*, as it's independent of the image's resolution. Typically used screen rulings are 65lpi for laser printers, 85lpi for newsprint, and 85–185lpi for high-quality paper stock.

Slurring

The effect caused by paper moving on press while a printing plate is making an impression. Images subject to slurring appear smudged with blurred *halftone* dots, and look as though the plate has skidded across the paper.

Soft proof

A soft proof is any digital proof viewed on a display rather than as a printed color proof. Professional graphics applications all offer the functionality to simulate on-screen how colors will be affected when different color settings are applied. The display used must be accurately calibrated if the results of soft proofing are to be relied upon.

Spread

A trapping technique in which a lighter-colored image or graphic object abutting a surrounding darker background is expanded outward slightly to create an overlap. (See also Trapping.)

sRGB

This color space has a relatively small gamut, and was created to provide a color space that represents a typical PC monitor. It's often the default color profile for consumer-level digital cameras, and is a viable option to choose when creating material for on-screen use despite its limitations when compared with the *Adobe RGB (1998)* color space.

Subtractive color mixing

Subtractive mixing happens when inks, or pigments, printed on any one type of surface (i.e. paper) absorb particular wavelengths of light depending on the pigments used. The resultant reflected light creates different colors, where cyan absorbs only red light, magenta absorbs only green light, and yellow absorbs only blue light.

SWF (Small Web Format or Shockwave Flash)

SWF is the proprietary *vector*-graphic file format produced by Adobe's Flash. SWFs are vector-based standalone files that can be highly compressed without loss of detail, and are completely scalable (because they are vector based), to the point that it's possible to create a full-sized browser window with a Flash-generated SWF file without creating large files. SWF image files can also contain audio and video footage, and are viewable with the Adobe Flash Player plug-in or standalone player. The fact that the end result is a fully self-contained file, with its own links and playback controls, makes the SWF format the ideal choice when presenting image slideshows, or when packaging collections of image content, such as portfolios and resumes. SWFs are embedded in web pages in the same way as an image, and work independently from the chosen web-authoring software.

TIFF (Tagged Image File Format)

A file format that combines both *bitmap* and *vector* and offers a number of different options for lossless compression when saved. It should be noted that some programs may not be able to import a TIFF saved with a particular type of compression unless a third party add-on is installed. The format is very flexible, but can take a relatively long time to print to a RIP due to the amount of processing required. However, its usefulness ensures its ongoing popularity with designers, and files can be saved as *RGB*, *CMYK*, *Indexed Color* or grayscale.

Trapping

Throughout a print run, registration between process colors will generally change very slightly. Trapping is a technique designed to compensate for this potential problem. Images, or indeed text and other graphic elements, are made to overlap slightly where they meet. This helps to avoid the appearance of gaps between separate elements of a layout where the paper color would show through. Generally, lighter colors are forced to extend into darker colors, depending on the trapping preferences set. (See also Choke; Spread.)

Undercolor removal (UCR)

A reproduction technique that removes excess or unwanted color from the shadow areas of an image. The process reduces the amount of ink used, providing better economy and helping to limit trapping issues. Colors that would otherwise cancel each other out in the *achromatic* system of color correction are also removed.

Vector graphics

Vector graphics allow the creation of digital images through a sequence of commands that place lines and shapes in a given space. Rather than including a "bit" in the file for each bit of a line drawing, a vector graphic file describes the series of points to be connected.

White balance

The term used to describe the digital control used to ascertain the correct exposure and color setting for images shot using artificial light. As well as an auto setting, and a setting for daylight, most cameras that carry a manual selection facility for white balance offer settings for tungsten and fluorescent lighting, flash, shade, and cloud.

White point

The point on an image's histogram that designates white pixels. Usually this point starts out at the far end of the histogram, but it can be adjusted back in Photoshop's Levels palette to correspond with the point at which the image's pixels are actually pure white, making the image brighter overall. In an *RGB* image the white point occurs where the pixels are at their maximum value; in a *CMYK* image it denotes the color of the paper.

The point at the beginning of a histogram is known as the black point, and designates the black pixels. Moving the black point slider to the right will make an image darker overall, particularly in the shadow areas.

Contributors

344 Design
www.344design.com

Absolute Zero°
www.absolutezerodegrees.co.uk

Accept & Proceed
www.acceptandproceed.com

appliance
www.designbyappliance.com

Black Eye Design
www.blackeye.com

Cahan Associates
www.cahanassociates.com

Cobra Creative
www.cobracreative.com

compoundEye
www.compoundeyedesign.com

Creative Review
www.creativereview.co.uk

Cyklon
www.cyklongrafik.net

Design Holborn
www.designholborn.co.uk

Fonda
www.fonda.co.uk

Forever Studio
www.foreverstudio.co.uk

Grade
www.gradedesign.com

Jason Keith
www.jasonkeithphoto.com

LEMON magazine
www.lemonland.net

Laki139
www.laki139.com

Loewy
www.loewygroup.com

Morris and Winrow
www.morrisandwinrow.com

My Poor Brain
www.mypoorbrain.com

+Plus
www.plus-design.co.uk

Simon Punter
photo@simonpunter.com

studio aka
www.studioaka.co.uk

Studio Output
www.studio-output.com

UMS Design Studio
www.umsdesign.com

Vault 49
www.vault49.com

With Relish
www.withrelish.co.uk

Useful links

www.adobe.com

For all things Adobe, this is the best place to start, particularly if you want to look at the available products and their features.

www.adobe.com/cfusion/exchange

This site carries a huge number of shareware and freeware extensions, scripts, actions and plug-ins to use with Adobe products.

http://labs.adobe.com

Not just for geeks, this is the place to go if you're interested in all the innovative new technology coming from Adobe.

www.apple.com

For all Apple software and hardware info.

www.color.org

The International Color Consortium site, with a wealth of useful information and links about color management topics.

www.enfocus.com

Enfocus develops specialist software for working with PDFs, so if you're serious about your PDF workflow have a look at the site.

www.extensis.com

The home of Portfolio, a justifiably popular digital asset management application which is well worth a look.

www.formac.com

Formac produce particularly good desktop and portable hard drives, and their monitors are excellent too.

http://creative.gettyimages.com

My personal favorite rights-managed picture library. Prices can be fairly high, but so is the quality, and they have a vast selection of royalty free images too.

www.indesignsecrets.com

Developed by "gurus" David Blatner and Anne-Marie Concepcion, if you need to know something about InDesign, you'll probably find it here.

www.istockphoto.com

An excellent and extremely cost-effective source for royalty free images. The quality of the material belies the pricing, which starts at just one dollar.

www.lacie.com

LaCie products are regarded by many professionals as the best of their kind. Their desktop and portable hard drives in particular are consistently voted top in user polls.

www.microsoft.com/Expression

Formerly iView MediaPro, Expression Media is now part of the Expression Suite

of creative software from Microsoft. Its basic functionality hasn't changed, which is great, as this application is my personal favorite for all digital-asset-management workflows.

www.photoshopuser.com

The site of the US-based National Association of Photoshop Users. There's lots of useful advice to be found here, and you don't have to be US-based to join up.

www.quark.com

The website of the venerable layout design application QuarkXPress, complete with updates, technical support, and training files.

www.russellbrown.com

Russell Brown is the Senior Creative Director at Adobe Systems Incorporated. His site is packed with useful tips, and refreshingly, doesn't take itself too seriously.

www.softpress.com

The makers of Freeway, the excellent web-design application that helps print designers like me feel at home with website design and layout.

www.vertustech.com

The developers of the very fine image cut-out tool Fluid Mask. If you do a lot of cut outs, take a look at this site.

Index

→ Index

→ Index

Acknowledgments

As a designer who works mainly in print, the preparation of the text for "Designing and preparing online projects" was a daunting prospect. I'm therefore very grateful to Rob Clymo for contributing so much to this particular chapter.

This project could not have been completed without the generosity and support of several companies and the individuals representing them. I would like to extend my sincere gratitude to all the people who helped me out, particularly Ginna Baldassarre at Adobe; Denise Duffy and Emma McDonnell at Quark; Simon Street at iView Mulitmedia and Kevin Bier at Microsoft; Claire Taylor at Extensis; Richard Logan at Softpress; and Steve Nelson at Vertus. Thanks also to Kelly Thompson and Megan Ironside at iStockphoto; Stephanie Hubbard at Getty Images; and Mia Garlick at Creative Commons.

My thanks to all the designers who contributed material to illustrate the text throughout the book—I hope that you're all pleased with the way I've represented your work. Also, for taking the additional time to provide me with their thoughts and insights for the Professionals' View pages, I'd like to single out Paul Burgess, Stefan Bucher, Peter Dawson, Russell Hrachovec, David Johnston, Jonathan Kenyon, Tom Morris, Patrick and Sara Morrissey, Ian Pape, Michel Vrána, Jane Waterhouse, and James Winrow.

Special thanks to Jason Keith for providing me with so much original photographic material to catalog, adjust, retouch, and generally mess around with. Thanks also to Lindy Dunlop, April Sankey, and all of my colleagues at RotoVision for their continual and wholehearted support, and to Steve Luck for his able editing of the manuscript and insightful advice.

I owe a great deal to my friends and family for their support throughout the whole of the writing and design process; no one could have offered more motivation, so a big thank you to you all.

And finally, for her endless patience, her constant encouragement, and for giving up so much her own time in order to help me put in the hours, I would like to thank and acknowledge my wife Sarah's part in this project. This book is also dedicated to her.